WHAT THEY SAY ABOUT
FINANCIAL SELF-DEFENSE

"Your specific advice on how one can shield their different assets is vital. What is even more important is how you think clearly and how it has helped me make smarter financial decisions."
— *H.B., Baltimore, MD*

"You've given our family peace of mind from the moment you first began to advise us. Your ideas have also inspired my other financial advisors to help their other clients plan more defensively."
— *Bill High, North Carolina*

"Your financial self-defense planning has been invaluable to both my business and my family's financial safety."
— *Scott Dantuma, Chicago, IL*

"I recommend Financial Self-Defense to anyone with the common sense to realize they could unexpectedly lose their assets in so many ways."
— *Alan Cohn, Esq.*

"I am now implementing your strategies. Even my family lawyer was surprised that he could gain so much practical knowledge from your book."
— *Brandon Miltsch, Atlanta, GA*

"You were always there for us when we needed you. We're delighted to see you share your wisdom with this wonderful, easy-to-read book."
— *Financial Forum, Florida*

"Insightful. Practical. Understandable. Now anyone can make sense of such a complex topic."
— *Chris Jarvis, CFP, Los Angeles, CA*

YOU COULD BE THE NEXT TARGET

THAT'S WHY YOU MUST ACT NOW TO:

- protect your assets against lawsuits and other financial threats
- achieve lifetime financial security for yourself and for your family!

READ....FINANCIAL SELF-DEFENSE...TODAY!
TOMORROW MAY BE TOO LATE!

FINANCIAL SELF-DEFENSE

HOW TO PROTECT EVERYTHING YOU OWN.... FROM EVERYONE... EVERY TIME!

Arnold S. Goldstein, JD, Ph.D.
Hillel L. Presser, Esq.

GARRETT PRESS

Financial Self-Defense
By Arnold S. Goldstein, J.D., LL.M., Ph.D. and Hillel L. Presser, Esq.
Copyright © 2009 by Garrett Press, Inc.

Published by Garrett Press
368 South Military Trail
Deerfield Beach, Florida 33442
Tel: 561-953-1322
Fax: 561-834-0295
www.garrettpress.com
e-mail: info@garrettpress.com

This publication is designed to provide accurate and authoritative information in
regard to the subject matter covered. It is sold with the understanding that neither
the publisher nor authors are engaged in rendering legal, accounting or other professional services. If legal advice or other expert assistance is required, the services
of a competent professional should be sought. From: *A Declaration of Principles
jointly adopted by a Committee of the American Bar Association and a Committee of
Publishers.*

Library of Congress Cataloging-in Publication Data

Goldstein, Arnold S. and Presser, Hillel L.
    Financial Self-Defense/Arnold S. Goldstein & Hillel L. Presser
p.   cm.
Includes bibliographical references.

1. Execution (law) – United States-Popular works. 2. Property-United States-Popular works. 3. D creditor-United States-Popular works. 4. Liability (law)-United
States-Popular works. I. Title.

This book is available in quantity or customized format for educational or
promotional purposes.
Printed in the United States of America   91-76105
10 9 8 7 6 5 4 3 2   CIP
ISBN: 978-1-880539-83-5

TABLE OF CONTENTS

ACKNOWLEDGEMENTS

From Hillel L. Presser:

This book is dedicated to the loving memory of my grandparents, Florence and Sidney. I'd also like to extend deep gratitude to my parents, Stephen and Suzanne, as well as my sister, Shifra and grandmother, Marcia for all the love and support they've shown me throughout the years. Although I've come a long way since I left upstate New York, I felt that you were all with me throughout my journey.

Very special thanks to my law partner and mentor, Dr. Arnold Goldstein. He's like my second father. Thanks to his lovely wife, Marlene, for her encouragement and continued belief in me. Also, my appreciation to my wonderful assistant, Barbara, for tolerating me and keeping me on track. Accolades to my friend, Elizabeth, for her book design.

Thanks to my friends for sticking by me – particularly Ron for his continued help and support. I can't say how much I appreciate your time and effort. You're truly my best friend.

Last, but not least; thanks to all my clients who have helped me as much as I have helped them.

From Arnold S. Goldstein:

First and foremost, my appreciation to my wife, Marlene, for her patience while I completed yet another book; and to my assistant, Barbara Schwartz, for poring tirelessly over the manuscript.

A special thanks to all my clients who have entrusted to me the safety of their wealth. I hope that I have served them well.

PREFACE

This book won't make you rich. Not another dime wealthier. But it can be the most important financial book that you'll ever read because it has an equally important objective: This book *will* show you how to *protect what you now own!* You will avoid becoming poorer!

That objective is vital in this day and age when the real trick is not to *make* money but to *keep* it!

The first goal of this book is to convince you that you must think and act defensively to keep your wealth safe. The book's broader mission is to reveal the many highly-effective strategies and tactics that we have successfully used to "judgment-proof" the assets of thousands of people against virtually every type financial disaster. Within these pages is the blueprint to build your own financial fortress so you and your family gain a comforting new level of financial security. And you can accomplish this more easily and with less expense than you might imagine. However, fortifying your wealth will take a seismic shift in how you now think about your wealth and how you financially plan. In sum, you must think and act defensively as your first step.

Why do so many people spend so much time and effort *building* their wealth, yet give so little forethought about how to keep it *safer?* It's true. Few people do *anything* meaningful to shelter their assets from life's inevitable financial disasters: lawsuits, bankruptcy, creditors, tax collectors, ex-spouses, foreclosure and so forth. The list of potential threats to your wealth is endless.

Who's safe from these and other financial reversals? Nobody. These troubles eventually strike each of us, and often when we least expect it. Until it does, we don't think much about *losing* our wealth. We simply strive to accumulate more. That's a huge mistake!

If that's you, you need a paradigm shift in your thinking for this book to help you. Accept our challenge. For every hour you work to *increase* your wealth, invest one minute thinking on how you might better *protect* it. Once you have your financial self-defense plan in place, make more money. You'll be building on a solid foundation.

JOIN THE
UNTOUCHABLES

You can use hundreds – if not thousands – of different legal and financial strategies to protect your wealth. This book explains the more common tactics and how to use them...plus many lesser known yet even more effective strategies that we asset protection advisors usually consider our own professional secrets. We want to share these little-known, seldom discussed strategies. This gives real value to this book.

What really works – and what doesn't – when you must shelter your wealth against a predatory attack? We'll tell you that too. No theory, but step-by-step strategies and "no-holds barred" inside facts as if you were in our office paying us hundreds of dollars an hour to get the same battle-tested advice you get here.

Showing you how to create *untouchable* wealth is only one of our goals. You'll also discover how to avoid the common mistakes and fatal errors that you may be making right now. These costly blunders can jeopardize your financial security!

Financial self-defense strategies range from the simplest to the most complex. You'll find no one correct formula or "magic bullet." Although we highlight the most effective, practical and common strategies, there are others beyond the scope of this book. Which is your best plan? That depends on the many factors unique to your own situation. For starters, it's enough to understand the broad overview and general concepts. Let's leave the technicalities and details for your lawyers. So use this book as your primer. An experienced asset protection lawyer can help you select *your* best strategies. Still, this book will highlight how you might more securely protect your assets and also make you that informed client who can work more effectively with your attorney.

This is one of several books on the important subject of asset protection. We have previously authored several best-sellers on the topic. However, this book approaches the subject differently from most other books. *Financial Self-Defense* presents the various protective strategies and shows you how to apply these strategies to each of your assets. This will help you to better understand your options to shield your home, investments, business, retirement accounts and every other asset that you own.

Some strategies won't be right for you. Each strategy is only one more possibility to consider. We emphasize that it's important to design *your* financial self-defense plan only *after* you consult with your attorney, tax, and other financial planners.

Financial self-defense planning has many dimensions. As dangerous as lawsuits and other predatory attacks are to one's wealth, you can also lose your wealth to inflation, a poor economy, bad investments and confiscatory taxes. To protect yourself from these wealth-robbers you need other solutions which we leave to other books. Still, some of our suggestions here may help you in these areas as well. This book then gives you a cornucopia of defensive ideas. You won't need them all. A few may meet your needs. But do bear in mind that any change to your financial affairs may have estate planning, tax and other consequences. That's why we urge you to involve your professional advisors *before* you act on any information in this book.

ESSENTIAL FOR EVERYONE
WITH VULNERABLE WEALTH

Financial self-defense isn't only for the wealthy. Anyone with *any* assets can benefit from this book. You need this book whether you:

- are that wealthy tycoon or have only a few assets that you wouldn't want to lose.

- are completely unprotected now, or *think* you're well-protected. You'll see how to begin the process of protecting your assets and how to improve upon your present plan.

- have never had financial problems, are now struggling with financial or legal problems, or want to be better protected against future threats.

- need to protect your own wealth or your client's. If you are a lawyer, financial advisor or accountant, you must accept the responsibility to improve your client's financial security.

- want to shelter personal assets or your business or professional practice.

- are starting out in life and want to safeguard your future wealth, or are in your twilight years and want to shelter your nest egg or your children's inheritance.

- hope to shield yourself not only against lawsuits; but also divorce, bankruptcy, bill collectors and any other financial hazard that could impoverish you and your family.

COMMIT TO YOUR FINANCIAL SECURITY... TODAY! WE ARE ONLY A PHONE CALL AWAY.

Put the ideas in this book to work for you. And to help you, we offer you a complimentary *Financial Self-Defense* Tool Kit. This includes an info-packed 2-hour *Financial Self-Defense* seminar on CD, a Wealthsaver® audit (to evaluate your risk and financial exposure), plus our e-mail newsletter. This $595 value is yours absolutely free. To register, visit *www.AssetProtectionAttorneys. com*. Or let us help you build your own financial self-defense plan. (contact us at 561-953-1050). Call us today, tomorrow may be too late!

We would be pleased to discuss your situation, explain our services and how we can work together to achieve your goals. There's no cost or obligation for this preliminary, confidential consultation. We accept clients nationwide – both individuals and companies.

CHAPTER 1

FINANCIAL SELF-DEFENSE

*The easiest job I have ever tackled is that of making money.
It is, in fact, almost as easy as losing it."*

– H.L. Mencken, Author, 1922

Objective: Planning for lifetime financial security.

DEVELOP THE
SURVIVOR MENTALITY

Everything in life begins with a good plan. This book is the beginning of your plan to build yourself a financial fortress – a literal barricade to safeguard your worldly possessions. With that accomplished, you and your family can live with some peace of mind. You'll have freedom from the fear that you might someday lose what you've worked so hard to accumulate. In sum, you and your family will have financial security.

Your starting point is to assess where you are now. What do you own? What are your financial concerns? What imminent dangers threaten your wealth? What have you done so far to protect your assets? How committed are you to a more secure future? Most importantly, how can you stop procrastinating and nonsensically pretending that the bad things that happen to so many others can't happen to *you*?

No, don't become paranoid. But do begin your financial self-defense planning with that one thought foremost in mind. You, too, *could* be victimized by a financial disaster. You may feel safe and secure today; however, your hard-earned wealth may end up in someone else's pocket tomorrow. It happens; and it's usually when and in a way you'd least expect. Endorse the old adage "Hope for the best, prepare for the worst." Common sense. Sure! It's vital to your economic survival in our lawsuit crazy, financially-perilous world.

TIPTOE THROUGH LIFE'S MINEFIELDS

The threats to your wealth come from many directions. Lawsuits drive most people to seek asset protection. While the causes of liability and litigation or other financial attacks are many and varied, however it happens, the danger of legal liability and potential financial disasters are always strong, regardless of your lifestyle, occupation or prudence. You can minimize danger, but youu can never fully avoid it. There are too many ways to get into trouble in our litigation-plagued, conflict-ridden society.

You'd likely agree that our legal system is out of control. The U.S. tort system is the most expensive in the industrial world. In fact, U.S. tort costs are 2.2% of the gross domestic product. Costs of litigation in the U.S. are *$867.37 billion dollars each year!* Our current civil litigation system is a monumental drag on our economy and burdens every American. It drastically increases the costs of services, goods, and health care, and forces thousands of Americans out of jobs each year when the companies they work for are forced into bankruptcy or massively downsized due to adverse litigation. Most dramatic is the estimate that 50 million lawsuits will be filed next year. Odds are about one in five that you'll be a target.

How can *you* be certain that you won't be hit with a breach of contract claim, bills you can't pay, a lawsuit from an auto accident or malpractice, creditor claims from a failed business, a whopping tax bill, divorce, foreclosure or governmental seizure of your property?

Since you can't guarantee your safety, your only logical option is to anticipate trouble. So protect yourself *before it's too late!* Develop that survivor mentality today!

GET THE MANY BENEFITS FROM YOUR OWN FINANCIAL SELF-DEFENSE PLAN

With a sound financial self-defense plan, you can be confident that you won't lose what you own, regardless of your legal or financial problems. Defensive planning does more than shield wealth. It discourages lawsuits. Those who are judgment-proof are a poor target for the contingency fee lawyers. "Deep pocket" defendants with exposed assets are their prime targets. Yes, you may get sued or run into other financial problems when you have your assets well-shielded; however, your financial self-defense plan gives you leverage to negotiate fast, favorable settlements once your adversary realizes how well your assets are sheltered.

The reality is that it's not *what* you own, but what you can lose to a claimant that determines your negotiating power. Protection = power! You can't control whether someone will chase your wealth, but you can – indeed, *must* – control whether they can *get* it.

The broad goal of asset protection is to provide lifetime security against threats to one's wealth. Exactly how asset protection accomplishes this objective is the subject of this book. But we'll show you other benefits from asset protection, including improved estate, tax, and retirement planning.

You may think that your protection only "kicks in" after a judgment is awarded against. But this is actually the exception, not the rule. Litigators acknowledge that 95% of all lawsuits are settled out of court. Settlements by their nature involve negotiating. The most effective negotiating involves psychological leveraging. And settlement negotiations are the crucible wherein most asset protection plans are tested. Asset protection is most effectively used as a psychological leveraging tool.

Financial self-defense planning is essential to any comprehensive financial plan. It enhances tax, investment and other financial goals. Integrating asset protection with your other financial objectives gives you a superior financial plan. Without *sheltering* your wealth, your financial plan is incomplete.

Is *your* financial plan complete? You wouldn't build your home without a roof. Why build your financial plan without a protective rooftop?

Keep these points in mind. Integrate the strategies in this book into your own financial plan and you'll not only better ward off serious threats to your wealth, but also title your assets in a manner that facilitates your other financial goals.

FORGET THE MYTHS AND FALLACIES, YOU NEED ASSET PROTECTION

Do you still think that you don't need this book; that you don't need protection; that you're too poor; that you have too few assets to protect; that you're too careful; that nobody would sue you? Nonsense!

Let's tackle these myths one-by-one. If you consider yourself too poor to need asset protection, how would you feel if you lost what few assets you do own? Wealth is relative. Your rusty old car and tiny bank account are mighty important when it's all you own. We get calls from people throughout the country worried sick about lawsuit or creditor problems. These hard-working folks sometimes have no more than a few bucks in the bank. Still, *their* wealth is precious to *them*. Protecting their few assets is as important as protecting a millionaire's millions! Wouldn't you agree?

The second myth is that you can't foresee anyone suing you. No, you don't need to be negligent, a lawbreaker or a deadbeat to lose your wealth. Life's a financial minefield. The most cautious and prudent among us get side-winded. Bad things happen that may not be your fault. And since bad things can happen to good people, they can happen to you!

We hear crazy stories about how suddenly someone's life has been turned upside down because of a lawsuit. Ask the 82 year-old client who accidentally drove her car through a supermarket window, or the landlord sued for lead paint on his old building, or the school teacher defending a $5 million lawsuit because she dismissed a student caught cheating on an exam.

These people never thought they'd someday get sued. One day they were going about their lives, and the next day they're defending against a claim from nowhere.

Life's unpredictable. Nowhere is it less predictable then when we talk about litigation or other financial hazards. You *think* you're safe. We know better!

DON'T STRICTLY RELY ON YOUR LIABILITY INSURANCE TO PROTECT YOU

Here's another fallacy: You figure that you can shield yourself by buying a big liability policy. You can't. Liability insurance is important. But liability insurance is only a *starting* point in your financial self-defense plan. It is not be your end point. Most lawsuits and other financial claims *aren't* insured, or you may have too little insurance to fully cover your claim, or your insurance company may deny you coverage on your claim because of some exclusion. Who knows, your insurance company may even go bankrupt. Some do.

The sad truth is that insurance covers few financial catastrophes. For solid protection you must do more than buy a liability insurance policy. You need a financial self-defense plan that protects you against *any* size or type claim…everytime!

MAKE FINANCIAL SELF-DEFENSE YOUR GREATEST INVESTMENT

You may hesitate to protect yourself because of the costs. So let's talk about that.

How much would you pay a good investment advisor to help you *build* your wealth? 1% – 1.5% a year? And you'll pay your advisor this fee whether he or she makes or loses money for you. You'll invest less to *protect* your wealth. And you'll invest this fee once, not annually. Most families can shelter their net worth for less than they'd pay for a modest vacation.

How much you'll invest on your financial self-defense plan, of course, depends on many variables. Yet, whatever you invest will be well-spent, particularly when you compare it to your net worth and what you spend annually for liability insurance.

Moreover, this book will show you many protective steps you can take that will cost you absolutely nothing. So don't think of asset protection as a costly, unnecessary expense. It's an investment, and it's your *best* investment! Talk to us. Let us estimate your investment for a lifetime of financial security for yourself and your family.

Cost is important when designing any asset protection plan. Don't spend more than absolutely necessary for your protection. On one hand, you want to spend as little as necessary for a certain level of protection, and on the other, you don't want false economy and end up with a faulty plan.

There are many low cost alternatives. For example, the foreign LLC oftentimes provides superior protection to the more expensive offshore trust. We can show you a number of judgment-proofing techniques (exemptions, tenancy-by-the-entirety, etc.) that cost little or nothing to implement.

Cost, of course, depends on both your plan and your planner. You can try to comparison shop different planners, but it's difficult to accurately compare. An offshore incorporation service, for instance, can set up a foreign entity for a lower fee, but does their entity have the most protective features? Do they include along with their entity legal advice or ongoing support? Do they integrate the entity with a multi-layered plan, or integrate the plan with your estate, business or retirement plan? Will they assist you with re-titling your assets into the entity, or do a risk analysis of your overall situation, help you avoid tax pitfalls, or even tell you whether you're using the *right* entity? Never compare apples and oranges.

The lower price provider may be no bargain. You can't simply *buy* a protective entity. It takes expertise to know structures and strategies will give you an optimal plan. Here's an artistry metaphor. More than colors on a palette create a fine painting. You must know how to apply the colors.

Compare the plans of different providers who have comparable credentials and who'll provide comparable services. A cost-effective plan should match the value of your assets against the cost of protection. How much should you spend to shelter assets worth $100,000? How much more for ten, or a hundred times as much?

CLEAR YOUR CONSCIENCE. SELF-PROTECTION IS NEITHER ILLEGAL NOR IMMORAL

You may question the *morality* of sheltering your assets against claimants. Believe us, we didn't write this book to benefit certified crooks or deadbeats. The law recognizes that honest, hardworking people have no moral obligation to gamble their wealth on life's financial vagaries. The law allows folks to *legally* shelter what we own. Bankruptcy laws, exemption laws, corporations, trusts and other protective entities and debtor-oriented laws are intended to shield wealth. Yes, you'll play by the rules and not break laws to achieve your defensive goals, yet the ethical question may still trouble you.

We each see things differently. You may think it's wrong to shelter your assets from those who assert a rightful claim. However, others sense no such ethical obligation. Why lose assets you can legally protect? Many lawsuits are meritless, inequitable or frivolous. Too many Americans are victimized by unfair, baseless claims. Life isn't without risk, but why needlessly participate in a legal lottery where you can unjustly lose what's yours on roulette-wheel justice? Hence our suggestion: If the ethics or morality about protecting yourself still concerns you, protect your assets. And if you feel morally bound to pay a particular claim; then pay. Appease your conscience and sense of fair play. Your defensive plan lets you deny wrongful claims. Without protection you lose that choice. You'll pay, period! Why unjustly lose everything you own to a claimant who has no conscience about taking *your* money. It's immoral *not* to protect yourself when it jeopardizes your family's financial security.

GET A GREAT
NIGHT'S SLEEP!

We are often asked: "Can I *really* protect my wealth…under every situation?" Nothing in life is 100% guaranteed. However, you can be well-protected *if* you protect yourself *before* troubles strikes… *if* you use the right strategies for your particular situation…*if* the right professional advisor builds your *financial fortress* …*and if* you *shelter* your wealth with the same strong commitment you have to *building* your wealth.

Put asset protection in the right light. A lawyer stubbornly pursuing the protected defendant can drag him or her through the courts. Nor should you assume you can fully protect every last asset. Some "loose change" will stay exposed. The ultimate success of any asset protection plan is not whether a plaintiff ends up with nothing. Even those who are fully protected often pay "something" to make their case go away. Your goal is to avoid losing *significant* assets. That's how we measure success.

We ask, "What more could we have done to get a better outcome for our client?" That's the litmus test for *any* asset protection plan. The true benefit of any financial self-defense plan is to reduce or eliminate the risk of *significant* loss. With that achieved, you can reduce your stress from the prospects of a major lawsuit or other financial upheaval. Defensive planning lets you sleep more soundly. That's *guaranteed!*

UPGRADE YOUR PRESENT PLAN WITH THE LATEST TECHNIQUES

You may already have a financial self-defense plan. Or *think* you do. You probably have only a *partial* plan, or a defective plan, or a tax-inefficient plan, or a plan that doesn't fit your other financial goals, or a plan that's no longer right for you. Thus, you don't have a coordinated, comprehensive, effective, updated plan.

Our planning starts by fixing, dismantling or upgrading your present plan. Most plans need fixing. It's not anyone's fault. There are many reasons for a plan's deficiencies. A plan designed for you years ago probably isn't your best plan today. Your personal and financial situations may have changed. So too did the strategies and laws. Your asset protection needs change as rapidly as your other financial needs.

So, it's time to have your plan reviewed. How can we improve it? You'd be amazed at the protective options available to you today!

INTEGRATE PROTECTION WITH YOUR OTHER FINANCIAL GOALS

Financial protection is only one financial goal. It isn't your only goal. You have estate planning, tax, and investment goals as well. So you need a coordinated, integrated financial plan.

For example, we integrate asset protection with estate planning. Most people needing asset protection also need an estate plan. Their need for asset protection may have prompted their estate planning. If you have a good estate plan, integrate it with asset protection. You have loads of opportunities to creatively combine protection with estate planning because both use similar entities and strategies.

Asset protection plans can also provide tax benefits. For example, a limited partnership that lawsuit-proofs your assets might also save you estate taxes. (Beware of promoters who use asset protection to push illegal tax schemes, i.e. pure trust, offshore tax savings, etc.). Make your planner explain the tax consequences of *any* proposed plan.

The primary purpose of your financial self-defense plan is to shelter your assets against financial and legal threats, but *how* you protect your assets largely depends upon your other financial and personal goals and objectives. So have your spouse and others affected by your plan consider the inevitable conflicts and trade-offs that your professional advisor should explain to you. Advisors cannot always sense your priorities or outcomes that are most important to you. Sometimes you must sacrifice one financial objective for another. That's why your financial planner, insurance professional, accountant and estate planner are equally important members of your financial planning team.

KEEP YOUR PLAN
100% LEGAL

Don't play games. Develop an absolutely legal plan. There can be that troublesome grey area between a legal and an illegal asset protection plan. But good planners don't rely upon secrecy, fraudulently concealed assets, perjury, tax violations, money laundering, bankruptcy fraud or defrauding creditors. That's not asset protection. That's commiting a crime!

A questionable or patently illegal "protective" strategy will only get you into bigger trouble. If you question the legitimacy of a proposed plan, talk to another planner. You have too many legitimate ways to shield your wealth without resorting to questionable practices. That's another good reason to avoid "do-it-yourself" asset protection. You can inadvertently overstep that legal line. You need a lawyer experienced in asset protection to keep you on the *right* side of the law.

GAIN LIFETIME
FINANCIAL PROTECTION

Nor can you protect your assets once and forget about it. Your finances will change, as will your obligations, the laws, the legal and financial hazards, and your financial goals.

So periodically review your asset protection plan, at least annually, and with each major event: windfall inheritance, threatened lawsuit, relocation to another state, family change, or new estate plan. Each triggers the need for review. Frequently update your plan and you'll have the most effective plan possible. Yes, it takes time, expense and effort to maintain strong, continuous protection; however, your protection erodes when you no longer consider protection a prime objective. Once you resolve a financial threat, you may consider protection less important. You'll then again become vulnerable. Losing protection can be as costly as never having protection!

IF NOT NOW
... WHEN?

Here's our most important advice: Protect yourself *before* trouble strikes. Courts and claimants *will* question asset transfers once a liability arises. Since you're reading this book, we assume that you recognize the potential dangers that could destroy your financial security. You have heard horror stories about people who lost their life savings, homes and businesses only because they were unprotected. If *you're* vulnerable, don't procrastinate. Procrastinators lose. Realists act *before* they're in trouble. They have peace of mind. They know their wealth is protected no matter what happens.

Do you and your family deserve less? Protect yourself now! *Tomorrow may be too late!*

CHAPTER 2

FINANCIAL
SELF-DEFENSE
STRATEGIES

What is financial self-defense or asset protection? Simply put, it's a strategy to title or encumber your savings, property, business and other assets in a way that shields them from lawsuits, creditors and other predatory threats. That concept is easy to understand, but asset protection is a much more complex process than most people, and even some planners, think. The less effective planners (unfortunately, too many) only address the "what do we do and how do we do it" aspects of asset protection. But, there are five dimensions to think about when constructing the truly effective plan: the *What*, *When*, *Where*, *How* and *Why* of asset protection.

How *can* you best protect *your* assets? There are countless ways. You undoubtedly know something about the more common options: exemption laws, LLCs, corporations, limited partnerships, offshore entities, trusts and so forth.

These strategies are only the tip of the iceberg. We have many highly effective "firewalls" that aren't commonly known, nor are they popularized in books or seminars. No, we can't discuss every possible firewall (though we do cover those that are most common and effective), but if you read our many asset protection articles and more technical texts that we wrote for lawyers, you'll see advanced methodologies. These sophisticated, "cutting-edge," legal and financial strategies and more complex arrangements can give you tremendous financial as well as protective benefits.

Asset protection isn't static. We asset protection planners constantly invent new strategies and tactics to perfect our science. Equally diligent plaintiffs' lawyers may find ways to pierce our newer strategies.

Some strategies are more financial than legal. For example, we employ structured financial products (SFPs), and complex arbitrage arrangements to effectively shift wealth between spouses with different liability exposures. Or we introduce a variety of domestic or foreign insurance products to better shield a client's wealth. Financial planning, as well as the available financial products, has become very sophisticated, and with it, the opportunities to design more effective asset protection plans.

To counter-balance complex plans are the quite simple, even obvious, plans. For example, exposed cash can prepay expenses or repay a favored creditor. Use common sense. It can give you your solution. Asset protection plans can be dissimilar because any plan is based upon many variables. How should you protect *yourself*? What is *your* best strategy?

Because asset protection is a new specialty, practitioners argue different theories and opinions as to the best approach in any given case. No two practitioners are likely to recommend the identical plan in a given case. Different approaches don't necessarily suggest that either plan is right (or wrong). Each planner – for whatever reason – simply believes her specific prescription is the best medicine. Ultimately, the test of *any* strategy is when debtor and creditor stand before a judge who decides which assets the creditor takes, and which assets the debtor keeps!

Strategy is more than choosing the right way to title your various assets. There's also the *timing* strategy. *When* do you build a stronger plan?

There's also the *jurisdictional* strategy. *Where* should you keep your assets for the strongest protection?

No less important is the *integrational* strategy. *How* do you incorporate asset protection into your existing or desired personal financial plan, or within your business's framework?

Strategy fundamentally involves doing "something" different with your assets. This involves dislocating your assets from its unprotected status quo. As you see, there are many variables to consider, so we can consider an incredibly broad range of strategic option. Though frequently, the options quickly become narrowed because the one best option is clear, or the circumstances (a pending lawsuit or imminent bankruptcy) reduce the possibilities.

This chapter gives you the broad strategic overview. Later chapters will show you possible strategies to shelter specific assets. The final section gives you tips to shield yourself in specific situations.

It's also important to separate principles from strategies, and strategies from tactics. Understand the principles. Know something about strategy. Think about tactics. But leave your final game plan to your advisor.

INVENTORY YOUR WEALTH.
THAT'S WHAT YOU COULD LOSE!

You're committed. You *know* you need protection. So, it's time to get down to business.

Assemble the financial information you'll need to create your blueprint. What assets must you protect? Inventory your wealth. Have your financial self-defense plan protect *everything you own*, and you probably own more than what might first come to mind.

Don't overlook your intangible assets, future assets, intellectual property, inheritances, monies due you, and so forth. These often overlooked assets can have great value. Download a convenient-to-use inventory worksheet at *www.AssetProtectionAttorneys.com*.

Estimate each asset's value. How is each asset titled (individually, tenants by the entirety, joint tenants, tenants in common, in trust, and so forth)? What percentage ownership do you co-own in each asset? What liens or encumbrances exist against each asset? What is the equity you must protect?

Review significant asset transfers that you made over the past five years so your advisor can decide whether these transfers can be recovered by your creditors.

Also anticipate inheritances and future windfalls that could come your way. They too need protection. Expand your inventory beyond your personal assets. Protect your business or professional practice, and never assume that a particular asset is already shielded and needs no further protection. Tell your advisor about *every* asset and let your advisor determine what needs more protection.

CUSTOMIZE YOUR
ONE BEST PLAN

We emphasize again that there's no "one right firewall," "one right strategy," "one right plan," or "magic bullet." You need a customized asset protection plan. What is best for you in your specific situation?

Since "one-size-fits-all" plans don't work, avoid "so-called" asset protection planners pushing that "one quick fix" or "magic bullet." For example, you can find plenty of assembly line planners who push Nevada corporations as "everybody's" asset protection answer. Others do only offshore trusts or limited partnerships. They oftentimes are good firewalls, but are they good for *you*?

Your asset protection planner must give you the widest range of protective options, because any one firewall is only one possible tool in the planner's toolbox. No one firewall is *everybody's* lawsuit-proofing answer.

Your planner must also *expertly* use each protective tool. Unfortunately, these more versatile planners are difficult to find. Few planners offer both offshore and domestic (U.S.-based) protective strategies. But high net-worth individuals frequently need *both* a domestic and offshore plan component. Your planner must skillfully provide both. Or your planner may protect only specific assets because that's how the planner makes money. Insurance professionals sell insurance/accounts receivable factoring programs to physicians and business owners, suggesting that through these financing plans they can protect their receivables against lawsuits. Such financed insurance programs *may* make sense for you. But even when it's good to shelter your accounts receivables, how will it protect your many *other* assets?

The planner who doesn't give you the complete arsenal of protective firewalls reduces your options and your protection. Your planner can only customize *your* best plan by considering every factor unique to you, including:

- What are your state laws?
- What assets must you protect?
- What liabilities do you need protection against?
- Do you need preventative or crisis planning?
- What are your financial (estate planning, investment and tax) goals and present plans?
- What strategies would you most comfortably adopt?
- What are the costs, both immediate and ongoing?
- What is your personal situation (age, marital status, etc.)?

We customize your plan by expertly blending these factors. Then it's only your best plan at that *point in time*. Your future plan may change.

SIMPLE CAN BE BEAUTIFUL, SO SIMPLIFY YOUR PLAN

No plan is good unless you can enthusiastically adopt it. Plans can be unsettling, particularly the overly-complex plan that you don't understand.

Complex circles and squares on your lawyer's legal pad are simple to your lawyer. But what do you really know about limited partnerships, offshore trusts, or captive insurance companies? Probably not much. So your planner must educate you. It's part of the planning process. That's another important reason we encourage you to thoroughly read this book, as well as other books on the subject. It's also why we urge you to attend our Financial Self-Defense® seminars. You must understand the various ways we protect wealth. Understand your plan and you'll become more comfortable with your new, more secure financial arrangement.

Some planners love complexity. They think it's the hallmark of a great plan. That's frequently untrue. Simplicity can be better. In fact, over-planning is a chronic error. Yes, we frequently "layer" multiple firewalls, but we can frequently get equal – or even superior – protection with a simpler plan. As importantly, a simple plan is easier for you and your advisors to understand. A simpler plan is also less likely to fall into disuse than a complex plan with its higher maintenance costs. The complex, high maintenance plan most often falls into disuse once a legal threat passes.

So, strive for simplicity. Make your plan more complex on an "as needed" basis, when a financial threat emerges and becomes more serious.

BUILD A FLEXIBLE, EASILY MODIFIED PLAN

No one plan is the most effective against *every* potential claimant.

Asset protection is like football. You need a defensive line that will best block a particular offensive line. So, how you'd protect your assets against a routine civil lawsuit might require a different strategy than one you'd use to protect yourself against divorce. A plan to protect against the small nuisance lawsuit would logically bear little similarity to one where a powerful litigant is suing you on a significant liability.

First and foremost, your plan must protect you against known, imminent threats; the danger that probably prompted you to seek protection in the first place. But you can't always foresee or anticipate your future troubles. So, start with a preventative plan, one that gives you a foundation or *basic* protection. Then add specific firewalls that would most effectively blockade specific threats as they appear. A flexible plan lets you more easily build upon or modify your plan to meet those future situations. Also understand your present plan's limitations, and consult your asset protection advisor whenever a new threat arises.

HAVE YOUR PLAN INSULATE YOU FROM LIABILITY

Your plan must also do more than protect your assets from claimants. It must also limit your personal liability. Your goal is to limit claimants to the fewest defendants and fewest assets possible. Avoid personal exposure. Title your assets to separate protective entities, so the creditors of any one entity can only target the assets owned by that one entity.

As a business owner or professional, you should not shelter only your personal assets – you must also protect your business. Limit creditors of any one business to the assets of that one business. Insulate each entity; then insulate each valuable asset within that entity. Planning must consider each *party, entity* and *asset* that needs protection.

ONLY OWN SELF-PROTECTED ASSETS IN YOUR OWN NAME

Back to basics: How can you protect your assets?

We mostly use one of three strategies, or "pillars of protection." The first pillar is to title only *exempt* assets to your personal name. The simplest way to protect yourself is to personally own only assets with federal or state statutory protection against lawsuits and creditors. These are *exempt* assets. Own no assets in your own name that are not exempt and self-protected. Unprotected assets owned individually are assets your creditors can easily claim. This book will highlight those assets that are most commonly creditor-sheltered. You usually don't need to do nothing more to protect them. Many people rely strictly on their homestead laws, wage and pension exemptions, bankruptcy exemptions and other protective federal and state laws to keep their individually-owned assets safe from creditors.

Four types of assets that are typically exempt:

- Personal residences (a.k.a "homesteads")
- Personal effects (such as furniture and clothing)
- Pensions and retirement funds (IRAs, 401(k)s, annuities, etc.) and
- Life insurance

To maximize your protection, you'd convert non-exempt (unprotected assets) into exempt self-protected assets. If you live in a more debtor-friendly state, you have several options. If you live in a less protective state, you might "jurisdiction shop" and relocate to a state that's more protective, or you might swap with a liability-free spouse your interest in *unprotected* assets for your spouse's interest in *protected* marital assets of equal value. But be careful. Transforming non-exempt assets into exempt assets has its limitations. In some states, "last minute" conversions are a fraudulent transfer if you already have a creditor.

How protective are these exemption laws against lawsuits? The answer varies by state. State exemptions can be extremely valuable or relatively meaningless. Exemption law efficacy depends not only upon what liability you need protection against, but also upon your state laws, your assets, and the equity in the asset to be protected.

Protecting yourself with the federal and state exemption laws can seem like a simple exercise, but it's quite tricky. You'll definitely need professional advice here, so you are confident that your state laws will fully protect your assets under *your* specific circumstances. You may have misconceptions about your exemption laws and assume certain assets are self-protected, but this may not be the case.

A greater difficulty with the exemption laws involves the interplay between the state exemptions and the federal exemptions (those which apply in bankruptcy). Pro-creditor changes in the new bankruptcy code have disadvantaged affluent debtors who will now find their state law exemptions less helpful if they go into bankruptcy. The homestead exemptions are one example. Conversely, the new bankruptcy law better protects certain other assets, most notably retirement accounts.

The threshold question in exemption planning then is whether you expect to resolve your legal problems with or without bankruptcy. Only when you have this answer can you determine which exemptions would apply. Nor can you always avoid bankruptcy. Because the new bankruptcy law is generally more favorable to creditors, we might expect more creditors to petition debtors into involuntary bankruptcy, causing these debtors to lose their more liberal state exemption protection.

A further complication is that not every state lets you apply the federal exemptions in bankruptcy, though most states allow a bankrupt individual to choose between the federal and state exemptions. (When you file bankruptcy you must choose exemptions. You cannot combine federal and state exemptions.) Though you must choose between the federal or state exemptions where you have the option, the exemption laws of certain states allow you to also apply supplemental federal exemptions, which may expand your protection.

You can choose which specific property to exempt within the terms of the exemption system that you elect. If you apply the federal exemptions in bankruptcy, you and your spouse may each claim the full exemption, but you cannot always double your exemptions under state law.

In either case, your strategy is to own as many exempt assets as possible. The states generally exempt the same assets that the federal system exempts, though their exemption limits vary.

You must then answer a number of questions before you design your one best exemption strategy. You may need both an asset protection attorney and a bankruptcy attorney familiar with your state laws. To conveniently find the federal and state exemptions, visit *www.bankruptcyaction.com/bankruptcyexemptions.html* .

PROTECTIVELY TITLE YOUR NON-EXEMPT ASSETS

Your next goal is to title your non-exempt assets to one or more entities that prevent your creditors from seizing those assets.

You have options. Co-ownerships, corporations, limited partnerships, limited liability companies, domestic trusts and offshore entities are a few possibilities. There are others. When you title your assets to one or more protective entities you sepa-rate your *legal* ownership from your *beneficial* ownership. You own only the beneficial rights – the rights to use and enjoy the asset. The legal ownership is with the entity which is not subject to your personal creditors' claims. Which protective entity will best shield a particular asset? That answer, too, depends upon several factors: the specific asset, your state laws, taxation, your estate plan, financing, the number of co-owners (if any), are a few. You'll need professional advice to choose your ideal entity. But we'll give you *general* recommendations for titling specific assets. Remember, other entities or strategies may be preferable in your case.

We often combine protective entities, whether to achieve more protection or to accomplish other planning objectives. For instance, you can multiply your protection if your limited liability company is owned by a limited partnership. As another example, your limited partnership may be owned by your living trust. This will give you asset protection (the limited partnership), and the living trust will let your estate avoid probate.

We discuss various entities throughout this book. There are other possible variations. Variations of limited partnerships are limited liability partnerships (LLPs) and limited liability limited partnerships (LLLPs). The potential entities to choose from and the various entities available from other countries can make your choice bewildering.

EQUITY-STRIP YOUR ASSETS

We must often do more than shelter non-exempt assets by titling them to one or more protective entities. We then have additional firewalls. One method is to "strip the equity" from real estate and personal property. Unencumbered, vulnerable wealth converted to debt-ridden wealth becomes worthless to a plaintiff.

We use many different mortgages and lien arrangements to equity-strip real estate or personal property. As the property owner, you or your protective entity retain title or legal ownership to the property, but you effectively transfer the asset's economic value to the mortgage holder; in this instance, to reduce the equity for seizure by creditors or litigants. Nothing discourages prospective litigants more than the reality that you are mortgaged to your eyebrows. You can own millions in assets, but if the mortgages against your assets equal their value, you are indeed a poor lawsuit candidate. Prospective litigants want equity to seize. When you pledge your assets to *other* creditors, your poverty becomes negotiating power.

Equity stripping for asset protection is its own specialized niche. We have developed many creative ways to structure "friendly" liens against assets. But you want bonafide liens. Sham mortgages can be set aside by the courts when you have a more aggressive creditor. You must also protect the loan proceeds. The devil is in the details. Again, that's why you need a good asset protection lawyer.

You'll notice that all of the above strategies fall into the category of either *transfer-based asset protection* (transferring an asset out of a creditor's reach) or *transformational asset protection* (transforming the asset into something a creditor couldn't get or wouldn't want). For example, part of your salary can be placed into an ERISA-governed plan (401(k), etc.) that is exempt from creditors. Although this involves exemption planning, it also involves transferring cash into an ERISA-governed plan, and is, therefore, transfer-based asset protection as well. Another method involves using exposed cash to prepay certain expenses or repay favored creditors (as long as those creditors aren't "insiders" under applicable fraudulent transfer or fraudulent conveyance law). For example, one could take exposed cash and use it to pay in advance for a five-year commercial lease. Such a technique results in the right to use an asset (the leased property), a right most creditors wouldn't want. This is transformational asset protection.

Nearly every asset protection strategy relies upon one or more of these three core strategies, while simultaneously utilizing either transformational or transfer-based methods. These are the "firewalls" from which you build your strongest financial fortress.

LAYER YOUR FIREWALLS TO CREATE MULTIPLE OBSTACLES

When in crisis planning (you already have claims against you), don't rely on only one firewall to protect your assets. No matter how safe or defensible the particular firewall, there's always *some* possibility it can fail. In dire circumstances, we "layer" protection with multiple firewalls. This is "belt and suspenders" planning. Should one firewall fail, others are in position behind it. We impose still more firewalls if and when they become necessary.

The challenge is to know *which* firewalls would be most effective in a given case, and *when* to interpose additional firewalls against the advancing threat. Asset protection planning frequently evolves in stages. The *preventative* plan advances to a *crisis* plan.

Plan *before* you incur liability and you'll probably need only a good preventative plan, or basic protection. This won't necessarily be your final plan if you're later sued because you may need something more for maximum safety against that particular threat. You then interpose those additional firewalls that would best protect you in that specific situation. Your goal is to become as judgment-proof as possible *before* you get a judgment against you.

Crisis planning is usually more costly and complex than a basic plan. That's why we usually layer additional firewalls only *after* a legal threat arises. Until that specific legal threat emerges, you can't foresee your one best defensive position. How you best protect yourself is greatly shaped by the claimant and how far that claimant will go to seize your assets. Other factors create what we call the case "dynamic." These, too, are factors your planner must consider when creating your optimum plan.

We usually start with a cost-efficient, simple, basic plan. Not everyone gets sued. Not every lawsuit is wealth-threatening. Or the serious lawsuit against you may be covered by insurance. You may quickly settle a lawsuit. Layer more firewalls in lockstep with the threat. To overbuild your plan prematurely costs you flexibility. Why incur needless cost and complexity only to later dismantle and reshape your plan?

Ultimately, your plan must give you the greatest possible safety. Still, no plan is guaranteed bullet-proof. If you have no legal problems, you may still want to know what your ultimate plan might roughly look like should it later become necessary. Our clients who are in litigation want to know what firewalls we might eventually use, when we would add them, and how and why each firewall works to help insulate their assets. It's important to understand your own ultimate financial self-defense game plan. Know your "end game."

Layering, or combining firewalls, exponentially strengthens your final plan. Layering builds strength into asset protection much as plywood is substantially stronger than the sum of its individual layers. To illustrate: a layered plan may combine a limited partnership, offshore trust, foreign LLC, and foreign annuity into one integrated plan. This interposes a formidable four-firewall barrier to stop all but the most persistent *creditor*. There are countless layering possibilities. This is *defense-in-depth*. The goal: make your creditor hurdle not one barrier, but multiple obstacles. Layering shifts the scale economics to you. It costs far less to build firewalls than to overcome them.

DIVERSIFY. SPREAD YOUR ASSETS AROUND

It's also smart to deploy your assets into separate protective baskets or protective entities. Why put your eggs in one basket? It can be a costly mistake. You want to force your creditor to pursue assets deployed in multiple directions, protected by different entities, and entrenched in several jurisdictions.

Scattering assets severely handicaps your creditor. If your creditor recovers assets from "one basket," the wealth sheltered in other "baskets" remains safe. Diversification is essential to protect significant wealth. For example, if you have millions at risk, we would deploy your funds into several protective baskets, which would also be quite dissimilar. Your "baskets" would be different protective entities (or entity combinations), and in different jurisdictions – whether states or countries. Combining layering (or *defense-in-depth*) with diversification (*defense-in-breadth*) produces a stronger shield.

CREATE PRESENT, FUTURE AND
FRACTIONAL OWNERSHIP INTERESTS

Here's another strategy: A curious thing happens when you divide your assets into present, future or fractional interests. The asset's value dramatically drops. In many instances, they become near-worthless to a creditor. So, rather than own assets outright, you may lease property with a long-term reverter (reversion of title) clause. Or you may own only a life estate to property. You have many ways to divide ownerships into time spans which can frustrate creditors who have nothing of substance to seize *today*.

Similarly, you can divide ownership (via a protective entity) between different family members or trusts. Co-ownerships (particularly tenancy-by-the-entirety in certain states) can also insulate the assets from claims against one co-owner spouse. Time-segmented, fractional ownership arrangements can also play a significant role in asset protection planning. These same techniques are also useful for estate planning, too. Combine these strategies with protective entities and equity-stripping to interpose another protective layer into your plan.

GO ON THE OFFENSE.
IT'S YOUR BEST DEFENSE.

There are a surprising number of ways to impose liability on a creditor who is after your assets. For instance, you can saddle a creditor with a charging order against your limited partnership or LLC with a huge tax liability. Or a creditor who starts litigation against *your* foreign trust or LLC may be forced to post a huge bond to cover your legal fees. We use these liability-imposing features as a porcupine uses quills. You become less attractive to predators. Counter-offensive possibilities seldom dictate using a particular defensive strategy, but it may influence it. You want your creditor to have a "downside" from pursuing you. A creditor uncertain about what he might gain from the asset chase must realize what he can lose. This sobering note helps level the playing field.

The best counter-offense strategy? Become so formidably protected that a creditor would incur huge legal fees to collect. The creditor's fees must be far beyond what the creditor can possibly recover from you.

Asset protection helps you win that war of attrition. Whether a plaintiff or defendant wins or loses is often decided by who must write out the bigger checks to their attorneys. That too is counter-offensive strategy. Don't go on the offensive only *after* your creditor wins a judgment. Go on the offensive when you're first threatened with a claim. That's your attorney's job. A good lawyer will know which tactics will make it painful (expensive, time-consuming, embarrassing, etc.) to chase you. If you don't have that kind of attorney, find one. You can't afford a milquetoast attorney – the type who knows only how to watch *you* get beat up while he sends you big bills. Your trial lawyer is your first line of defense. Your asset protection lawyer plays back-up. He or she is your safety net. If you are in serious litigation or your wealth is otherwise in jeopardy – and your defense attorney doesn't suggest an asset protection safety net, it's time to wory about how "street smart" your lawyer really is.

Defense-in-depth, diversification, and counter-offensive planning adds more complexity and cost to a plan. Therefore, some of these strategies may not be appropriate for you if you have a lower net-worth or if your assets are not at immediate or serious risk.

RETAIN CONTROL
OVER YOUR ASSETS

Another common perception about asset protection planning is that one must always surrender control over their assets. That's sometimes true. However, it's frequently untrue. Much depends on the specific firewalls.

For instance, the limited partnership and limited liability company are two entities that let you retain complete control, and the assets titled to these entities will remain protected. Similarly, one would retain control over exempt assets and assets titled between husband and wife as tenants-by-the-entirety. Other methods allow you to control your assets while having little or no apparent control to recover assets from the structure. An example would be to title your cash to an offshore LLC that purchases an offshore variable annuity. You retain control how the cash is invested inside the annuity. However, the annuity policy governs when, how much, and to whom annuity payments are made. You can take it a step further, so you have no unilateral ability to withdraw annuity payments (after they've been made) from the offshore LLC (although you may exercise that right with the consent of an offshore manager or co-manager). These measures are important if it's necessary to prove your inability to repatriate assets to the U.S. per a judge's order, for example.

On the other extreme, it's fatal to a plan if you retain actual or *defacto* control over a trust created to protect your assets. Even then, there are various control retention techniques that should allay most of your fears about delegating control to a third party.

A good plan strikes an optimum balance between safety and control; an objective not always easy for a planner to achieve because many clients stubbornly want to retain full control over their assets, even when it endangers their plan. While it's possible to achieve strong protection without sacrificing control, you'll find that there are preferable ways to safeguard your assets even when you must entrust them to others. You gain considerably more planning options once you understand these control mechanisms, and a plan can be customized for you that will give you greater control, or even complete control, while still adequately protecting your assets.

How much control you can safely retain in any given instance must, of course, be determined by your advisor, and it's always wisest to err on the side of caution. Oftentimes a debtor has little choice but to relinquish control.

BUY LIABILITY INSURANCE AT HUGE SAVINGS

More about liability insurance for protection. Liability insurance is a sound planning strategy. But too little insurance coverage still exposes you to judgments above your coverage. Considering that plaintiffs' lawyers manipulate juries into bizarre awards, you can't predict what a litigant can recover. Your million or multi-million dollar liability policy may not be *enough*. Excess liability claims or lawsuits for more than the insurance coverage are escalating. Most cases settle within the liability policy limit. But until your case settles, you'll suffer the anguish that possibly – just possibly – you may be hit by a judgment above your coverage. You'll then lose your assets, despite your insurance.

Less than a million dollar liability policy is inadequate. But insurance is expensive. You must buy it right to get *maximum* protection at *minimum* cost. Some tips:

■ *Segregate the costs for each liability policy.* One coverage may have tripled in cost while other coverages have decreased. Which coverage remains a good buy and which should you reduce or eliminate?

■ *Increase your deductibles.* Absorb whatever losses you can to reduce your premiums substantially.

■ *Utilize free programs.* For instance, insurers reduce auto insurance premiums when drivers enroll in drivers' education classes.

■ *Check if your trade or professional association* can deliver substantial savings with their sponsored liability insurance.

■ *Investigate package policies* if you own multiple businesses. It can reduce your premiums by 25%.

■ *Shop.* Insurance rates are regulated in only several states. Get five bids and re-bids annually. Who's this year's lowest cost insurer?

With your premium savings, buy an umbrella insurance policy. Umbrella insurance is essential for every family, individual or business. An umbrella policy protects you against claims not covered by standard insurance policies, as well as claims beyond standard policy coverage, such as homeowners and motor vehicle insurance. A $2 million umbrella insurance policy costs relatively little. Check with your insurance agent.

DOUBLE YOUR PROTECTION IF YOU "GO BARE" WITHOUT INSURANCE

We don't always recommend insurance. Liability insurance is one reason for many costly, frivolous lawsuits. Insurance means "deep pockets," and deep pockets attract lawsuits. Litigants know insurance companies have money and that insurers often settle frivolous lawsuits because defending a case can be far more costly.

Insurance not only attracts lawsuits, but it's also prohibitively costly for doctors and others in high-risk industries who can less afford its escalating costs. That's why so many professionals and business owners "go bare" without liability insurance. One obvious problem with dropping your liability insurance is that you must then pay your defense costs if you're sued. It can easily cost you $100,000 or more to defend against even a routine liability or malpractice suit, so going without insurance can also be expensive. If you "go bare" (or uninsured), then obviously you greatly increase your need for solid asset protection. So buy legal defense fund insurance to cover your defense costs. Combining legal defense coverage with a good asset protection plan can be a sound alternative to huge insurance premiums which only magnetize lawsuits.

CHECK OUT STRUCTURED FINANCIAL PRODUCTS

Not every financial self-defense strategy is taught in law school. Some of the better strategies are taught in business school.

For example, structured financial products (SFPs) (which range from more speculative investments to complex arbitrage arrangements) can, in a variety of ways, depress (on paper, at least) the value of your investments. This reduced value essentially transfers into a protective entity. Creditors can, only with great difficulty, unravel these transactions. The wide array of possibilities (and their complexity) makes them difficult to fully explain, but zero-coupon bonds, staggered calls, collars, puts and other arbitrage, replication or devaluation procedures are common techniques. These strategies aren't important if you have modest wealth. Yet they're essential to the planning for high net-worth individuals with large portfolios and sufficient financial sophistication to understand their plan. We work closely with financial planners to create smart financial solutions to meet our clients' wealth-sheltering needs. Insurance professionals and insurance-based products are also valuable tools in our arsenal. More and more asset protection lawyers now use financial products in their planning. These financial products can also advance the clients' investment or estate planning goals.

BEWARE OF TITLING YOUR ASSETS TO YOUR SPOUSE

You have seen the more common strategies. Now let's discuss the mistakes and costly errors that only weaken or destroy your protection, create problems, and can cause you to lose your assets.

Here's such a mistake: "I don't need asset protection. My assets are titled to my spouse. As a housewife, she won't get sued." Chauvinism is politically incorrect. Nor is it always true that the stay-at-home wife (or husband) is invulnerable. More wives are breadwinners. Our point, however, is that it's bad strategy to title marital assets to the less-liability-prone spouse. This common strategy has obvious hazards. Can you be certain your spouse will stay creditor-free? Divorce is also common today. Although divorce courts normally equitably divide marital assets, regardless of which spouse holds title, the spouse holding title may sell, mortgage or conceal the assets. And when the marital assets are titled to one spouse, you lose a huge estate tax reduction opportunity (your estate tax exclusion). Moreover, creditors can argue that the assets were purchased or maintained with the debtor-spouse's funds, so the non-debtor spouse holds these assets in constructive trust for the benefit of the debtor-spouse and derivatively the claims of his or her creditors. The law works in curious ways. Titling assets to your spouse is seldom your best option.

NEVER DO "STRAW" OR NOMINEE DEALS

You don't title your assets to your spouse. Instead, you figure that your easiest, safest option is to title your assets to a trusted friend or a relative until the legal threat against you passes.

Why do people foolishly believe that a "straw" is their "best" strategy? The "straw" holding your property may be a friend or relative, but whoever it is; they hold title to your assets. The real deal, of course, is that you still own the asset. But for lawsuit protection, you don't want the asset in your name.

The pitfalls to this are apparent. First, it's a fraudulent conveyance to gift assets to a friend or relative without consideration, on the tacit understanding that they'll return your property once your creditor goes away. Think about it. Nominees or straws have their own marital problems, tax troubles, creditors and lawsuits. Will a straw's creditors or ex-spouse claim *your* assets? You can as easily lose your assets to your straw nominee's creditors as to your own.

The tax problems are also significant when you title your assets to individuals other than your spouse. It triggers gift and capital gain taxes. Your nominee straw can also incur a gift tax when he or she re-transfers the property back to you. And bankrupt individuals who title assets to straws have bigger troubles. Bankruptcy fraud is a serious crime.

Finally, can you *really* trust your straw? Who can you *really* trust? Parents steal entrusted assets from their children, and siblings double-cross siblings. Your best friend might forget that *your* asset isn't really his. Avoid straw deals! We can show you far safer and legal ways to protect your assets.

WHY HIDE YOUR ASSETS?
SELL YOUR PROTECTION

Never confuse secrecy or concealing assets with asset protection. Financial privacy can be helpful, but once you're sued you can no longer rely upon secrecy because a judgment creditor can compel you to disclose your assets. If you truthfully disclose your assets, you lose secrecy. If you conceal your assets, you commit perjury. That's not legitimate protection. You want a plan that lets you fully disclose your assets, confident that they'll remain safe from your creditor. A judgment creditor can force financial information disclosure through deposition, interrogatories, requests to produce documents or subpoena your records and information from third parties.

Judgment creditors can and do find debtors' assets. Loan and credit applications, bank records, tax returns, court cases (such as prior divorce that discloses assets) and insurance policies all provide clues. The paper trail is revealing. Computers expose our financial lives. Judgment creditors and prospective litigants often use professional asset search firms to find concealed assets. These firms can financially profile you with stunning accuracy. Forensic accounting firms trace deviously and secretively deployed wealth. So avoid "hide the assets" games. Your creditor will probably find your assets.

The sounder policy? Tell your claimant early in the game exactly what assets you own and how they are titled. Most importantly, explain precisely why they are beyond creditor reach. Make asset protection your selling tool. Convince a claimant that you're simply *not* worth suing.

The cold hard reality of litigation, from an attorney's perspective at least, is that it's almost always all about money. Attorneys work for a living. They have bills to pay like everyone else. Although they often represent clients on a contingency fee basis, they'll normally do so only if they believe they'll get paid. If a potential defendant has no exposed assets, the attorney won't get paid. Most plaintiffs' attorneys first do an asset search on a potential defendant before taking on a contingent fee case. If their search reveals few unprotected assets, the attorney is then uncertain whether he will get paid for his efforts. Even if the asset protection plan is pierced, the process may be lengthy, expensive, and uphill. The attorney will then insist on an up-front retainer before accepting the case. This shifts the risk of suing a defendant and losing (or being unable to collect) to the plaintiff, who now realizes their lawsuit can be an expensive, risky undertaking!

Other than lawsuits with the potential for large judgments against wealthy (albeit asset protected) individuals, attorneys and would-be plaintiffs usually opt for easier prey. This is basic human (and even animal) nature. A pack of predators stalking a herd go for the easiest kill.

With that said, people who think they are well-protected may not be. The predator/litigant determines that an apparent defense is only smoke and mirrors. The defendant is surprised to lose his or her assets. They learned too late that you can't have illusory protection. You need solid, effective asset protection!

As asset protection planners, we see many well-protected clients threatened with litigation, only to have the threat fizzle. The effectiveness of protection is most striking when several co-defendants are sued. The protected clients are dropped from the suit which proceeds full-steam against the unprotected, deep-pocket defendants.

DON'T LET FRAUDULENT TRANSFERS UNDERMINE YOUR PLAN

Books have been written about fraudulent transfers. Mention asset protection and you'll have questions about this important topic. It's not necessary to become an expert on fraudulent transfers, but you should know the basics. Your asset protection plan can't become that sound financial fortress unless it can withstand a fraudulent transfer claim – an especially important point if you have already been sued or have a present liability.

Asset protection planning is a vaccine, not a cure. The only sure way to avoid fraudulent transfer claims is to protect yourself *before* you're in trouble. Once you have a lawsuit or liability, many otherwise protective strategies are no longer effective – just as a vaccine loses effectiveness once you are afflicted with a disease. The best protection is *preventative* planning.

The fraudulent transfer laws give claimants the right to unwind or revoke certain transfers made by debtors so that the transferred property can be seized by the judgment creditor. In other words, under certain circumstances, the courts invalidate sales or gifts by debtors. Whatever the debtor sold or gave away is transferred back to him or her, so the creditor can seize the property. These laws prevent debtors from transferring property to defraud their creditors. A fraudulent transfer can partially or totally destroy your protection. For sound protection, you must title your wealth free of these potential claims. Fraudulent transfers are obstacles to that goal because creditors can recover assets no longer in your name. Fraudulent transfer laws distinguish effective protection from the ineffective disposition of assets.

Judgment creditors use fraudulent transfer laws to reach assets transferred to a spouse, family member, friend, corporation, partnership, trust or any other third party. Creditors succeed when they convince the court that the transfer was a last-ditch effort to defraud them. So a fraudulent transfer challenge is often the true test of an asset protection plan. To recover, the creditor must prove: 1) there was a gift or transfer of property, 2) for less than fair value, and 3) which left the debtor insolvent. This, of course, greatly simplifies what is in actuality a complex law. There are often differences of opinion between lawyers and courts as to what, constitutes a fraudulent transfer.

The fact that a creditor might, recover a fraudulently transferred asset doesn't necessarily mean that every creditor tries. Few fraudulent transfers are recovered by creditors. One reason is that few judgment creditors discover fraudulent transfers, or the amount owed the creditor, or value of the transferred assets, may be too small to justify the creditor's time and expense to attempt recovery. Moreover, there may be many competing creditors, and recovery by one creditor isn't worthwhile to that creditor when the creditor must share the recovery with other creditors. Finally, the procedural obstacles to recovery may be too great. For example, offshore asset protection imposes procedural barriers that make it extremely costly and time-consuming to attempt recovery.

A creditor then may have legal recourse under the fraudulent transfer laws as a *theoretical* remedy, but they might not find it their *practical* remedy when they must overcome too many firewalls. The creditor's *legal right* to reclaim fraudulently transferred assets becomes academic when the creditor won't assert those rights in practice, but this shouldn't encourage fraudulent transfers. Also, it's faulty to base your plan upon the mere hope that a fraudulent transfer won't be discovered or acted upon by a judgment creditor. The best plan is one where your creditors can't recover assets as a matter of law, and *won't* attempt recovery as a matter of practicality.

This doesn't suggest that it's too late to attempt to protect yourself once you have been sued. It does mean that you'll have fewer good options, and that your resultant plan may be somewhat less effective than one completed before you incur liability. The greatest danger to your financial safety may be the lawyer who tells you that "nothing can be done" because you have already been sued. True, *fewer* things can be done. But until your assets are already seized by your creditor, you do have options. Also remember, a fraudulent transfer is not a crime. It is simply a creditor remedy to recover assets.

Planning delves more into the "why, when and under what circumstances assets were re-titled to their now safer refuge." Courts don't want their judgments ignored, and they're less cooperative with debtors whose last minute shenanigans put their assets out of harm's way. Then there's that tactical question about how and why your plan came to be. We must convince a judge that your plan had an innocent purpose. It must essentially pass a "sniff test" that doesn't offend judicial sensibilities. Here's where the asset protection planner meets the greatest challenge.

STAY CLEAR OF
FRAUDULENT TRANSFER BADGES

A transfer is fraudulent if made "…with actual intent to hinder, delay, or defraud any creditor of the debtor." There's no bright-line rule here. A judge looks for indicia or "badges" of fraudulent intent. A judge has broad discretion in determining whether the presence of one or more badges indicates a transfer was fraudulent. Furthermore, the standard of proof that must be met to indicate fraudulent intent is not the "beyond a shadow of a reasonable doubt" standard of criminal trials. But rather it is the less rigorous "preponderance of evidence" standard of civil litigation.

The potential badges you should avoid include:

1. *The transfer or obligation to an insider:*

   This may, or may not, be a factor in determining whether there was a fraudulent transfer. For example, it's common business practice for someone to transfer personal property to a business they control (such as an LLC, LP, or a closely held corporation) in order to capitalize it. Such a transfer, if done while creditor seas are calm, will almost certainly not be considered fraudulent, especially if the transferor receives an interest in the company equivalent to their capital contribution. On the other hand, transferring real estate to one's uncle the week before a lawsuit commences will likely be considered fraudulent.

2. *The debtor retained possession or control of the property transferred after the transfer:*

   This may or may not be a factor in a fraudulent transfer case. For example, although a lien is a transfer of equity, mortgaged real estate typically remains in the owner's possession as a matter of standard business practice. In contrast, placing one's home in an offshore trust and then continuing to live in it rent-free is more likely to be seen as a fraudulent transfer.

3. *The transfer or obligation was concealed:*
   See the comment for badge of fraud (7) below.

4. *Before the transfer was made or obligation was incurred, the debtor had been sued or threatened with suit:*

   Some transfers (such as a gift to an insider) are very vulnerable to a fraudulent transfer ruling if they occur after a creditor threat arises. At the same time, no judge would expect you to stop your normal business activities once you've been sued, especially considering that a lawsuit may drag out for years. Of course, some business activities may involve transfers of assets. Consequently, if you are facing a lawsuit, it's important to transfer property so there is a plausible reason for the transfer, besides trying to protect assets. For example, by taking money and investing it in an LLC, you can protect the money while honestly claiming that you were only engaging in a business venture, instead of trying to defeat a creditor. At the same time, your claim of having a valid business purpose may be insufficient if other badges point to the fact that you transfered the asset to hinder, delay, or defraud your creditors.

5. *The transfer was substantially all of the debtor's assets:*

   The most important consideration here is the need to avoid insolvency through a single transfer. Assuming one remains solvent, it's a good idea to stagger the implementation of an asset protection plan over time. For example, don't equity-strip all your rental units on the same day. Instead, interpose a few months between transfers.

6.   *The debtor absconded:*

   This is a very strong badge of fraud, which by itself would probably cause a transfer to be deemed fraudulent.

7.   *The debtor removed or concealed assets:*

   Oftentimes, there's a good reason for financial privacy, besides trying to defeat a creditor. Depending on your reasons, it may not be safe to conceal assets while the creditor seas are calm. However, this is usually not a good idea once one is threatened by creditors. Remember: everything can and will usually be revealed in court, and privacy is more for lawsuit prevention than anything else. Above all, remember that no plan should rely exclusively on secrecy and that improper (but not all) financial privacy measures are usually considered a badge of fraud.

8.   *The value of the consideration received by the debtor was not reasonably equivalent to the value of the asset transferred or the amount of the obligation incurred:*

   This is why trusts are sometimes (but not always) a poor choice for protecting assets, since property is typically gifted to the trust. However, it's possible to transfer assets into a trust in a manner that involves an exchange of equivalent value. This badge demonstrates that gifting in general is usually a bad idea from an asset protection standpoint. In contrast, when someone transfers an asset to an LLC, they receive an LLC membership interest in return. Done correctly, this membership interest constitutes an equivalent value of consideration received for the transfer.

9.   *The debtor was insolvent or became insolvent shortly after the transfer was made or the obligation incurred:*

   Implementing an asset protection plan and then failing to pay one's debts as they become due, whether through inability to do so or otherwise, is a big error. Continue to pay at least most of your debts.

It's important to realize that these badges are not black and white indicators. A judge is given wide latitude to interpret the types and number of badges present when considering whether there was a fraudulent transfer. Only rarely will a single badge denote a fraudulent transfer, whereas in other situations multiple badges of fraud won't be enough to prove fraudulent intent. Regardless, any asset protection program should avoid these badges whenever possible.

Above all, remember a judge must determine whether a particular transfer was undertaken to cheat a creditor. If there's not a plausible economic reason for a transfer, and if the transfer is not a part of "business as usual", then it might not stand up if challenged in court. Such transfers will almost always carry at least one badge of fraud.

OBSERVE SIX RULES TO AVOID FRAUDULENT TRANSFER RULINGS

Because fraudulent transfer rulings are so detrimental to asset protection, it's a planner's highest priority to structure their plan so, to the extent possible, they can avoid the likelihood of such a ruling. Here are six strategies that can effectively help you achieve this.

1. *First and foremost, get your assets out of your name while the creditor seas are calm, even if the transfer is to a very simple structure.* As long as the entity itself is not a debtor, a subsequent transfer by that entity will not be considered fraudulent. Accordingly, when a creditor threat arises, you can then reinforce the entity or transfer the asset to

a new entity with reduced fraudulent transfer concerns. The reason for this is that the law considers only transfers the debtor makes as potentially fraudulent. Furthermore, restructuring an entity so that a creditor of the entity's owner cannot reach the entity's assets for its owner's debts usually doesn't involve a transfer, and is, therefore, not considered a fraudulent transfer in most states. Even if it did, as long as the entity is not a debtor, a transfer from the non-debtor entity to another entity is usually not considered fraudulent.

2. *Build up assets in a structure. Since these assets were never yours to begin with, there is no fraudulent transfer issue, period!* This approach works best with an income-producing business or investments. For example, if you own a business, instead of transferring all profits to yourself, have another entity own the business. You can then take enough money from this entity to pay your cost of living, and the rest can remain in the entity where it can be invested. Because this money remains inside the entity, the assets never comes into your possession. Consequently, if you're sued there's no fraudulent transfer issue, period!

3. *If you implement asset protection after a creditor threat arises, make sure that you receive an asset of equivalent value in exchange for your transfer.* The trick here is to receive an asset that is exempt from creditor attachment in exchange for your transfer. Or you could purchase an asset a creditor couldn't otherwise touch (such as an offshore annuity held in a properly structured offshore entity). Remember, under the law you have to not receive an equivalent value for your exchange *in addition to being insolvent* for a fraudulent transfer to have occurred (unless, of course, a creditor can prove the transfer was done with intent to delay, hinder, or defraud the creditor.

4. *In addition to avoiding the badge of fraud in (3), avoid other badges of fraud whenever possible.* Not all transfers carry badges of fraud, even if the transfer incidentally protects the asset from creditors. For example, if you were to trade in your old car for a new, expensive leased vehicle, this transfer of cash for the lease (which will have little value to a creditor) will almost certainly not be considered a fraudulent transfer, even if badges of fraud (4) (making the transfer after creditor threats materialized) and (9) (making a transfer while insolvent) are present. As long as the transfer is a bona fide business transaction for equivalent value with a truly independent party, badges (4) and (9), are much less relevant (nonetheless, we should still avoid these badges of fraud if at all possible).

5. *Do you have other creditors who are not insiders? If so, and you come under creditor attack; then pay your non-hostile creditors.* This is an excellent tactic that works even after creditor threat has arisen. The U.S. Supreme Court has noted that "In many [states], if not all, a debtor may prefer one creditor to another, in discharging his debts, whose assets are wholly insufficient to pay all the debts."

6. *If creditor threat has already arisen, then use a proper offshore plan to purchase a foreign annuity. This transaction will likely be protected.* Although strategies (3) and (4) (above) minimize the likelihood a fraudulent transfer ruling, they don't completely eliminate it. Furthermore, strategies (5) and (6) may not protect all of your assets, or may not be feasible. Therefore, if the strategies we've discussed up to this point are inadequate, and creditor threats already loom, consider offshore planning.

This is, in many instances, the ultimate wealth protection plan. Protecting your money offshore in foreign trusts and/or LLCs insulates it from the U.S. court orders. Buying a foreign annuity through these entities is a fair value exchange which would put the transaction beyond the scope of a fraudulent transfer. You'll see this strategy in greater detail in later chapters.

BUILD A PLAN
THAT WORKS

Everything else is meaningless if your plan doesn't achieve its primary purpose to protect your assets. No planner can guarantee the absolute safety of their plan (and be wary of any planner who does); however, you want at least reasonable certainty that your assets can sustain a creditor attack should it occur. Ultimately, you want your assets as close to 100% lawsuit-proof as legally possible. Anything less is *not* a great plan.

CHAPTER 3

FINANCIAL
SELF-DEFENSE
FOR YOUR HOME AND OTHER REAL ESTATE

Your home may be your most valuable asset. It's likely the one asset you would most hate to lose.

Home is where you live. Home is where you raise your family. Home is your refuge against the world. Our homes are very much part of us. We are emotionally attached to what we call "home." How can we keep it safe so that it's never at risk? Fear of losing one's home stems not only from the many foreclosures and the credit crisis, but also from the reality that we can lose our home to "garden variety" creditors – litigants, credit card companies and other unsecured creditors who may see your home equity as their easiest asset to claim.

What about your other properties? Many families have second homes and vacation properties. Real estate investing has accelerated in the past decade or two, so you may own several, or a great number of investment properties, or you might own the building your business occupies.

How should you shelter each property? How can you shield yourself (and your other properties) from liabilities each property may generate? How do you keep each property untouchable from claimants, such as litigious tenants? Let's begin with your home.

MAXIMIZE YOUR HOMESTEAD EXEMPTION PROTECTION

Protecting your home starts with your homestead protection.

Five states completely homestead protect the family home; however, most states only partly creditor-shield the home. States with homestead laws vary greatly in how much home equity they protect. Five states have no homestead protection.

The homestead laws apply only to your home or *primary* residence, property that you own *and* occupy as your home, and that you consider your domicile. But which specific "residences" qualify for homestead protection depends upon your state statutes and court rulings. For example, some states shelter only single-family homes, not duplexes or multi-unit structures. Will your state laws homestead protect a mobile home or houseboat that you use as your "home"? Interesting question!

The next question is how much home equity will your homestead laws protect? Compare the statutory protection against your home equity. Subtract the mortgages against your home's fair market value. For example, a $300,000 home with a $150,000 mortgage has $150,000 equity. If your state homestead protects $20,000, then you have $130,000 equity vulnerable to lawsuits and claimants.

Follow the procedural requirements to claim homestead protection. Each state sets its own requirements for homestead protection. Some states' residents must file a declaration of homestead in a public office. Other states impose a residency period before they grant homestead protection. Don't assume your home is protected. Let your attorney help you comply with your state's procedural formalities. Some states permit only the head of the household to claim homestead protection; however, most states extend homestead protection to either or both spouses.

Nor will your homestead exemption shield your home against every creditor. Homestead laws ordinarily protect the home only against debts incurred *after* you claim homestead protection. Moreover, certain creditors can override your homestead protection:

- The IRS (and some other federal agencies following special procedures). If you owe federal taxes or are sued by the SEC or the EPA, for example, you can lose your home, regardless of your state laws. Your homestead laws may or may not protect your home against the state tax collector.

- Ex-spouses in divorce or family members challenging their inheritances.

- Plaintiffs with claims for intentional torts (libel, fraud, deceit, etc.).

- Lenders holding a consensual lien (a mortgage) against your home, or creditors to whom you specifically waived your homestead rights under a contract.

Your goal is to maximize your homestead protection. Some states let spouses apportion their exemption so the liability-prone spouse may claim more of the exemption. If your state has an unlimited or large homestead exemption, you might pay down your mortgage with exposed cash (to convert the cash into protected equity), or use the cash to improve your property.

Some debtors jurisdiction shop and relocate to a state with broad homestead protection. But a word of caution: You must own and reside in your home for 40 months before you file bankruptcy or your homestead protection caps at $125,000; regardless of your state law. Converting unprotected cash to increase your homestead-protected equity is another complex area of law that relies largely on your state laws plus bankruptcy law which has, under the new bankruptcy laws, greatly reduced your strategic options.

Homestead protection can be illusory. For example, if you now own a $30,000 home equity with a $30,000 homestead exemption, your home is *now* fully protected. But will your home be protected in the future as you build equity (assuming your home appreciates) while you reduce your mortgage? If you're sued some years from now, you will have substantially more equity to lose. Your present creditor can sit on their recorded judgment against your home until there's enough exposed equity to satisfy their claim. Because of its limitations, the homestead exemption seldom sufficiently protects the family home. The best strategy is to periodically refinance your home so that your mortgages *plus* your state homestead exemption leaves no exposed equity available to creditors.

MARRIED? CO-OWN YOUR HOME AS TENANTS-BY-THE-ENTIRETY

You may have heard the term "tenancy-by-the-entirety?" This special type joint tenancy is for spouses in 25 states. The tenants-by-the-entirety laws (T/E) in several states gives you about the same creditor protection as joint tenancy, that is, very little. However, assets that spouses title as tenancy-by-the-entirety in other states are well-protected against lawsuits.

In more protective tenancy-by-the-entirety states, a creditor of only *one* spouse cannot claim that debtor-spouse's interest in property owned by the spouses as tenancy-by-the-entirety (T/E), though a creditor of *both* spouses can claim tenancy-by-the-entirety property. For example, if both spouses guarantee a bank note, the bank could claim the tenancy-by-the-entirety property. However, if only one spouse is sued on a debt, then tenants-by-the-entirety property would be lawsuit-protected from that one creditor. You can see the value of this protection.

Does your state have T/E protection? Check *www.AssetProtectionAttorneys.com.* If T/E protection can shield your home and other assets, then discuss it with your attorney. Re-title marital property now held jointly to tenancy-by-the-entirety. Other than improved asset protection, titling the home as T/E works in the same manner as joint tenancy, which includes rights of survivorship.

Tenancy-by-the-entirety laws unevenly protect different assets. Some states limit tenancy-by-the-entirety protection only to real estate, or the family residence. Florida and New York have strong tenancy-by-the-entirety protection laws which can safeguard the home and any other asset. In these states, you may safely title most everything you own, including your home as tenancy-by-the-entirety. But most tenants-by-the-entirety states partially lawsuit-protect assets. For example, Massachusetts protects the T/E titled family home from the creditors of one spouse for the period the other spouse resides there, but not thereafter. Tenancy-by-the-entirety laws provide patchwork protection. You must know which assets the T/E laws in your state protect, as well as its exceptions and limitations.

Tenancy-by-the-entirety protection is hardly bullet-proof. For example, if you and your spouse own property as tenants-by-the-entirety and your spouse suddenly dies while you have a judgment creditor, you would immediately inherit the entire property, which could then be seized by your creditor. Divorce also extinguishes tenancy-by-the-entirety. Divorcing spouses might logically transfer tenancy-by-the-entirety property to another protective entity before they divorce (particularly if one spouse has creditors), but ex-spouses don't always cooperate. The IRS can also disregard T/E protection.

Finally, avoid tenancy-by-the-entirety (and joint tenancy) if you do not want to bequeath your property to your spouse. For instance, if you are in a second or third marriage, you may want to instead bequeath your assets to your children. Tenancy-by-the-entirety defeats this possibility, as will joint tenancy. How you title your assets has estate planning as well as creditor-protection consequences.

SIDESTEP LIENS AGAINST YOUR HOME WITH A SINGLE MEMBER LLC

It's often wise to title your home to a single member limited liability company because the home titled to the LLC avoids a judgment creditors' attachment from clouding the home's title.

The limited liability company and family limited partnership can both protect assets. But we wouldn't ordinarily title the home to a family limited partnership or multi-member limited liability company (though some asset protection planners do title the family residence to a limited partnership). The downside is that you lose your home ownership tax benefits that you keep if you title your home to a *single-member* limited liability company which is a disregarded entity for tax purposes. The limited partnership is not.

A single individual has $250,000 capital gains tax exclusion on realized profits when they sell their home. If you title your home to a family limited partnership or multi-member LLC for more than 3 out of 5 years, you'll lose your homeowner tax benefits. You could transfer your home to a family limited partnership for less than 3 years and then retransfer your home back into your own name for at least 2 years, but this can be impractical and expensive. The better alternative: title your home to a *single*-member limited liability company. If you're married, the less-liability prone spouse may be that single-member. Since the IRS disregards single-member limited liability companies for tax purposes, the home, for capital gains purposes, should be treated as if owned directly by the individual member. You can't use this tax-preservation strategy with a limited partnership, which requires two or more partners and thus is not a disregarded entity. Review this with your tax advisor.

Why do we recommend this strategy? Suppose a creditor wins a judgment, which, if recorded, would cloud your home's title. If you previously titled your home to the LLC, its title would be unaffected by the filed judgment. The judgment would be against *your* name as the *prior* owner. This doesn't necessarily extinguish the creditors' rights as the creditor might try to reverse the conveyance as a fraudulent transfer. Single member LLCs are also sometimes liquidated by the courts when the only member is the debtor, but including a second member would lose the LLCs status as a tax-disregarded entity. Therefore, you need careful planning to coordinate your tax and asset protection goals. But generally, if you keep your home equity protected by homestead and mortgages, titling it to a single member LLC can then keep its title clear of personal judgments filed against *you*. Remember that a transfer to an LLC may cause you to lose your homestead protection.

PROTECT REAL ESTATE OWNED AS TENANTS IN COMMON

Aside from your own home, never own any other real estate in your own name. And never own real estate with anyone as tenants-in-common. When each tenant-in-common owns a divided fractional interest in the property, this creates serious lawsuit dangers and offers you, the co-owner, no creditor protection.

Consider the risks. Suppose you and your friend John own an apartment building as tenants-in-common. You or John can sell, gift or mortgage your half interest in the building without the other's consent. You are "partners" in the business of renting apartments. As tenants-in-common, you and John each own a separate half interest in the building. Your interest is separate from John's. Your creditors cannot claim John's interest. John's personal creditors can claim only *his* half-interest. Your share of the property is safe from John's creditors, but not your own. This might seem to be an acceptable risk if you consider yourself a *safe* co-owner, yet tenancy-in-common can still cause huge problems.

For instance, John's personal creditors could force the sale of the *entire* property to satisfy John's personal debts. You might buy John's interest to avoid this forced sale, but this may not be practical or possible. If the property is liquidated, you'll lose the property, though you will recover your half the sale proceeds. John's creditors might acquire John's half-interest in the property.

You would then have a new and unintended partner, John's creditor! It happens. John's financial problems *can* become *your* problems and your problems, John's. Nor is *your* ownership interest safe from your own creditors. If John's creditors can seize his interest, your creditors can seize *yours*. Co-owning property as tenants-in-common is always risky. Avoid it. Title your real estate to one or more protective entities. You can own the respective interests in these entities as tenants-in-common.

Tenancy-in-common also *expands* your potential liability. For instance, John may accidently injure somebody by negligently managing the co-owned property. You and John will *both* get sued since you co-own the property. If a plaintiff wins a judgment for more than the property's value, *you* may pay because you and John as co-owners are jointly and severally liable for *every* debt from the co-owned property. Bottom line: Don't directly co-own real estate as tenants-in-common.

Some larger commercial properties are owned by multiple owners as tenants-in-common. It might be sloppy organizational planning. Probably it's because the co-owners want a Section 1031 tax-deferred IRS exchange of the property. To qualify, they must directly own the real estate. If that's your situation, make certain the property carries adequate liability insurance to protect you. Avoid guaranteeing loans or other obligations that *you* as the deepest pocket defendant may have to pay. With Section 1031 exchange property, you must better protect your tenancy-in-common interest against your personal creditors. You may, for instance, title it with your spouse as tenants-by-the-entirety, or encumber it, or reduce the value of your co-interest through options. There are solutions.

BEWARE OF DANGEROUS
JOINT TENANCIES

Joint tenancy is another form of co-ownership distinguished from tenants-in-common in several ways. One is the right of survivorship. When a joint tenant dies, the jointly-owned property passes to the surviving joint tenant(s). Jointly-owned property passes outside a will, which avoids the expense and delay of probate. For this reason, financial and legal advisors often encourage their clients to jointly co-own their real estate (and other) assets when the parties want these assets to pass to the surviving joint-owner. These advisors don't always advise their clients how joint-ownership can hurt them. Joint tenancy is a frequent mistake. It significantly increases your lawsuit exposure, frustrates sound estate planning, and gives you little or no lawsuit protection.

Jointly-owning personal property or real estate carries the same lawsuit and creditor consequences as tenancy-in-common. You aren't lawsuit protected because your creditors can seize your interest in the jointly-owned property, just as your co-owner's creditors can seize theirs. If your co-owners(s) creditors seize your co-owners' interests in the property, the creditor becomes a co-tenant in common with you. A co-owner's creditor can also force the sale of the entire property to recover debts owed by one debtor co-owner, though the creditor can claim only the sale proceeds due the debtor joint owner. You also have the same tenancy-in-common liability risks.

Joint-ownership is a "winner-takes-all" game. You "gamble" that you'll survive your co-owner (joint tenant). Because jointly-owned property automatically passes upon death to the surviving joint tenant(s), if the liability-free co-owner dies before the debtor co-owner, the entire property passes to the debtor and can then be claimed by the debtor-owner's creditors. For example, if you and John jointly own a building and you die, John inherits the entire building. Your family loses further ownership claim to the building. Joint tenancy then impairs estate planning. If you want to gift the property to your children, you would normally provide for this in your will or living trust. Jointly-owned property instead passes title by rights of survivorship to your surviving joint tenant(s). You thus effectively disinherit whatever beneficiaries are designated in your will or trust to inherit your jointly-owned property interest.

We commonly see this avoidable tragedy. Folks don't always understand this survivorship feature about joint-ownership. Their advisors never inform them. People in dangerous joint ownership arrangements don't realize their risks or consequences of the arrangement. Others have little idea how their assets are titled, and fewer understand the consequences of the various co-ownership arrangements.

Like tenancy-in-common, joint tenants are jointly and severally liable for debts or liabilities arising from the co owned asset. This expands their liability.

How is your property titled? Do you own your property jointly (or as tenants-in-common)? See your lawyer! Title the property instead to a protective entity. If you want your interest in the property to pass to the surviving joint owner when you die, then jointly own the entity with title to the property.

REDUCE YOUR ESTATE TAXES AND PROTECT YOUR HOME WITH A PERSONAL RESIDENCE TRUST

Time for a potential tax-saver and asset protector – all in one!

A Qualified Personal Residence Trust (QPRT) is a special type of trust. The grantor transfers his or her primary residence or vacation home to the trust while retaining a tenancy in the residence for a term of ten years. After the 10-years, the residence passes to the trust beneficiaries, usually the children. The objective: transfer the residence while it has a lower value rather than when you die and it has a higher value. The QPRT then helps you reduce your estate taxes.

QPRTs also provide good asset protection. As the grantor, your creditors can claim only your rights to *use* the property for the remaining term of years (or claim the rental value for those years). But this would be of little economic value to your creditor. The beneficial remainder interest cannot be claimed by the beneficiaries' creditors if the trust has spendthrift provisions. At the end of the term, the trustee must distribute the residence (or cash proceeds from its sale) or convert the QPRT into an annuity. This is preferable in those states that creditor-protect annuities and where the beneficiaries have creditors.

You can transfer vacation properties to a QPRT (but not other non-occupied investment properties). If you die within the 10-year term, the property reverts to your estate for estate tax purposes. If you survive the ten years, the property passes to the beneficiaries.

However, a transfer to a QPRT can be a fraudulent transfer if you have present creditors. You then need additional safeguards, such as equity stripping. But consider a QPRT if you have a rapidly appreciating primary or secondary residence and a taxable estate, you are in your later years, and you want asset protection as your secondary goal.

SELL AND LEASE
BACK YOUR HOME

When your home is imminently threatened by creditors, it can sometimes make sense to sell the home and lease it back. Protect the cash proceeds from the sale as you protect other cash assets, using the strategies from the next chapter. Link the lease with an option to re-acquire the property at some later date. Have this option held by a third party acting on your behalf, or an entity that can exercise the option and re-acquire the home.

Debtors with serious or chronic creditor problems shouldn't own a home or other properties – whether individually or indirectly through an entity. They should temporarily give up the idea of home ownership, or instead title their home to a debt-free spouse. Of course, the ultimate asset protection plan is to simply lease *everything*.

When you can honestly explain to a claimant that you own *nothing*, it's one sure way to dissuade further chase. The elderly are less concerned about "ownership" and building equity. They prefer simplicity, lifestyle flexibility, and the liquidity from leasing rather than owning. It's a mindset. In a sense, we all lease our assets. No one takes their assets when they go! It's a good philosophy to remember when your assets are in some creditors' cross-hairs.

GET A LINE OF CREDIT AGAINST YOUR HOME

Homestead protection and protectively re-titling your home may not fully protect your home equity.

Your third strategy is to mortgage your home to the hilt to reduce any exposed equity. "But I don't want a big mortgage," you argue. "Why pay interest on a loan that I don't need to protect myself against a lawsuit that may never happen?" Good question. Refinancing your home may *not* make *financial* sense, but it can make *legal* sense. That's why we recommend *home equity* loans. For example, if your home is worth $200,000 and you have no mortgage, you could probably get a $150,000 home equity loan or line of credit against your home (75% to value). You'll owe your lender nothing until you draw against your credit line, which you would do only if you anticipate a judgment.

Think of its advantages. A prospective litigant on an asset search would see only $50,000 equity in your home as the $150,000 line of credit mortgage would be public record. You become a less attractive defendant because you significantly reduced your apparent net worth or equity. You lower your exposure to *future* lawsuits, and you gain leverage to negotiate a favorable settlement if you do get sued.

You can get a line of credit against *any* real estate. Have your equity loan or line of credit cover as much equity as possible. Get a standby second or third mortgage to encumber any additional exposed equity. You'll pay loan processing fees, but your line-of-credit will prove a great investment for lawsuit protection.

TITLE YOUR INVESTMENT REAL ESTATE
TO LIMITED LIABILITY COMPANIES

We almost always title real property, other than personal residences, to an LLC. Properties owned by an LLC cannot be claimed by your personal creditors because the property is owned by the LLC, rather than you personally. Your personal creditors also cannot seize your membership interest in the LLC. Your personal creditors can only get a charging order against your membership interest. The charging order liens whatever future distributions are due you from the LLC. As the LLC manager, you are not liable personally for LLC debts. This is why LLCs are preferable to limited partnerships to title investment real estate. General partners of a limited partnership are personally liable for LP debts. You can solve this problem by using a corporation or LLC as the general partner, but it's simpler to bypass this cumbersome dual structure by using an LLC.

In addition to titling commercial property to LLCs, also title your second home and vacation properties (even time-sharing units) to an LLC. Title *all* real property, other than your primary residence, to an LLC.

How do LLCs work? Limited liability company statutes vary; however, the model Uniform Limited Liability Company Act (ULLCA) provides:

- A limited liability company is a legal entity separate from its members.

- Limited liability companies may be for-profit or non-profit.

- Some states allow one-member limited liability companies; others require two or more members.

- Limited liability company membership interests are non-transferable without the unanimous consent of the other members.

- A member may transfer his or her interest in future distributions and returns of capital.

- Managers and members of a limited liability company have limited liability. They can lose only their investment if the limited liability company is sued or goes bankrupt.

- Limited liability companies can be for a fixed or perpetual duration.

- A limited liability company is dissolved upon: 1) the consent of its members; 2) dissociation of a member; 3) occurrence of those specific events stated in the operating agreement; or 4) a fixed dissolution date.

- Limited liability company operating agreements may not: 1) unreasonably restrict a member's right to inspect company records; 2) eliminate or reduce a member's duty, loyalty, care or good faith when dealing with or on behalf of the company; 3) restrict the rights of third parties; or 4) override the legal right of the company to expel any member convicted of wrongdoing, breaching the operating agreement or making it impractical for the limited liability company to carry on business with such a member.

- You can avoid double taxation with a limited liability company. Since the limited liability company is not a corporation, you can avoid corporate income tax if you choose. Income from the limited liability company can be taxed personally to its members as with a partnership.

■ Members are personally protected from limited liability company creditors – even when the members participate in managing the company. General partners of a limited partnership are personally liable for partnership debts, and limited partners of a limited partnership cannot manage the limited partnership without incurring personal liability.

Due to its organizational advantages, the LLC is now the primary choice to title real estate, other than the family home. If you title your investment properties to a corporation, your stock in the corporation can be claimed by your personal creditors. Avoid this danger. Use an LLC. Think about converting your S corporation to an LLC. But structure this correctly since the conversion may carry tax consequences. Discuss this with your tax advisor.

TITLE EACH PROPERTY TO A SEPARATE LLC

A good asset protection plan titles each property to a separate LLC.

If you own five rental properties, title each to a separate LLC. Liability from one property won't jeopardize your other properties. Similarly, operate separate businesses through different entities to accomplish the same objective of liability insulation. So why not your real estate too? Real estate investors oftentimes have hundreds of separate LLCs owned personally or through one or more limited partnerships, which adds one more layer of protection, as well as providing estate tax discount opportunities.

Your LLCs may also be owned by one or more trusts, such as a living trust or offshore trust. If you own several small properties or properties with no significant equity, you can combine these properties into one LLC. But generally, it's best to segregate your properties to limit liability and the risk of loss arising from each property.

NEED MULTI-LLC PROTECTION?
CHECK THE SERIES LLC

Of course, you must be organized and separately administer multiple LLCs.

To simplify matters, Delaware and several other states have a newer entity, the Series LLC. A Series LLC includes a series of "cells" within the LLC. Each cell functions as a distinct LLC. Each cell can own different assets, conduct different businesses, have different managers and members, and adopt different operating agreements. Each cell can file separate tax returns, and in most other ways, operate autonomously from the other cells within the series. Most importantly, the liabilities from any one cell are segregated to that one cell. Assets titled to the other cells stay safe. Consider the Series LLC if you need multiple LLCs. More states will soon adopt Series LLC legislation.

Though the Series LLC is a new entity (thus far, only a few states have Series LLCs) you can register your Series LLC to do business or hold property in any state. A lingering problem with the Series LLC is that lenders, title companies and attorneys are still unfamiliar with this type of entity, and it can then be more cumbersome to use. Another significant question is whether states without Series LLC laws will respect a Series LLC and segregate liability to the respective cells. Most planners expect that the Series LLC liability insulation *will* be respected in non-series states, but thus far, there's no case law. For this reason, if you do use a Series LLCs in non-series states, additionally reinforce the assets within each cell as an extra precaution. Encumbering the various properties is the common solution.

BULLETPROOF YOUR LLC

You want a bulletproof LLC, as you want with any other entity used for asset protection.

If you have a "do-it-yourself" LLC, you'll need a well-drafted LLC operating agreement for this protection. This point you might overlook. You may not understand the importance of a bulletproof operating agreement and have a less protective LLC.

A surprising number of creditor-proofing provisions can be added to your operating agreement, and they will greatly enhance your protection. Have an asset protection attorney review your operating agreement and modify it to include every possible safeguard.

Generally, a limited liability company member's personal creditors cannot seize or force a sale of the member's interest. Nor can the creditor claim the limited liability company's assets. Nor can a member's personal creditor vote the debtor-member's interest. The member's creditors can only have the court issue a charging order to instruct the limited liability company to pay the debtor's income distributions to the creditor. This is the same "charging order" remedy that a creditor has against a limited partner's interest in a family limited partnership. The creditor gains only the *financial* rights of the debtor-member, not *control* rights.

The charging order doesn't give the creditor voting rights or force the limited liability company manager to pay distributions to members – or their creditors. The charging order only requires that any distributions payable to the debtor-member instead be paid to the creditor.

The charging order is as futile a creditor remedy with a limited liability company as with a family limited partnership. If you manage your limited liability company, you determine the distributions. Your judgment creditor cannot vote you out as the manager because a member's creditor can't vote as long as your creditor has a charging order against you. As the manager, you can refuse to make distributions. You can compensate yourself and other members through salaries, or withdraw money as loans, or take other compensation.

"Poison pill" the charging order remedy. A charging order backfires on a charging order creditor for income tax purposes. A limited liability company is ordinarily taxed as a partnership, so its tax liability passes directly to its members. But, in most circumstances, a charging order creditor is taxed for the debtor-member's share of the profits. Think about it. A member's creditor pays taxes on earnings the creditor never received!

These, and other problems and limitations with the charging order, usually encourage creditors to settle rather than fight. Why sue for a remedy that assures no money, no control and the possibility of a large tax bill? A plaintiff's lawyer, who knows at the outset of a lawsuit that your property is titled to a limited liability company, probably will settle fast and you'll avoid the expense and time of litigation.

The limited liability company's weak point is also the same as the family limited partnership's. Assets you transfer to the limited liability company *after* you have the liability may be recoverable as a fraudulent transfer. Further, a bankruptcy trustee has greater rights to claim the member's limited liability company ownership interest than does a judgment creditor who is limited to a charging order. Also, profit distributions may be made if the debtor-member doesn't control the LLC's management. These are factors to consider.

You can improve your protection for your limited liability company. Follow the same strategies you would use to increase the protection of your corporate shares and limited partnership interests. Examples: assess the membership interest, issue proxies and options to redeem the membership interest, encumber or lien the membership interest, or dilute the members' control by selling additional ownership interests. Also it is important for the operating agreement to impose executory obligations on its members. This provides considerably more protection for a member's interest if the member files bankruptcy. The point: It's not enough to form an LLC. The real protection is in its operating agreement. You need these and other protective provisions in *your* operating agreement.

HAVE A LIMITED PARTNERSHIP OWN YOUR LLC

Here's how to double your protection.

If your LLC owns substantial real – estate or if your LLC includes non-family members – you'll need stronger protection. To directly own your LLC membership interest subjects your LLC distributions to your creditor's charging order. If your LLC has multiple members, or if the LLC is managed by a manager who controls distributions, have your LLC interest owned by a limited partnership that you do control. An even safer arrangement? Set up an offshore trust to be the limited partner of the limited partnership. This completely insulates any profit distributions from the LLC.

Limited liability company's membership interests owned by spouses may be titled as tenants-by-the-entirety in states that protect this type of marital ownership. We particularly recommend a limited partnership as the member of a limited liability company in those states that provide greater creditor protection to limited partnerships than to limited liability companies.

A limited partnership owning your limited liability company also reduces your estate taxes. To improve protection, add members to the LLC who are not co-defendants in your lawsuit. Courts won't expand upon a creditor's remedy when other members would be affected. Conversely, courts will more likely liquidate an LLC when the debtor is the sole member, since no other members would be hurt.

GAIN MORE PRIVACY. TITLE YOUR REAL ESTATE TO A LAND TRUST

The land trust can camouflage your ownership interest in real estate.

Land trusts, popular in Illinois, Florida, Georgia, California, Colorado and other states, can own any real estate, including the family home. Land trusts can be used in any state. The land trust's chief benefit is secrecy, not protection. But since secrecy aids protection, it's useful in your planning. A bank ordinarily is the land trust's trustee. As the trust beneficiary, you wouldn't directly own the real estate. It would instead be titled to the trustee. You would own only a beneficial interest in the trust. This interest is considered personal, not real property.

Owning a beneficial interest in a land trust does not, in itself, give good protection. For protection, title your beneficial interest in the trust to a limited partnership, an LLC, or an irrevocable trust. Privacy, not asset protection, is the land trust's main advantage and chief selling point. Beneficiaries of the trust are not public record because the property is titled to the trustee.

Land trusts have disadvantages. It can be difficult to finance trust property since the trust property must be temporarily reconveyed to its grantors or beneficiaries for financing. Also if you, as a beneficiary, want a Section 1031 tax-free, like-kind exchange, you must transfer the property back to yourself from the trust, since a land trust beneficiary doesn't own a beneficial interest in real property but only an interest in personal property. Layer your protection. Have different land trusts own different properties. Use different LLCs to be the beneficiaries of each trust. Have each LLC, in turn, owned by a different limited partnership or protective trust. You have a number of structuring possibilities. Finally, you may fully encumber the trust's properties.

MORTGAGE YOUR INVESTMENT PROPERTIES, TOO

Back to that great strategy of fully encumbering your assets.

You see why it's important to equity strip your home. But it's good strategy for *any* real estate. Get an equity loan or line of credit to cover as much equity as possible in your properties. Then arrange for standby second or third mortgages to encumber any still exposed equity. The challenge, of course, is to find a lender who'll fully equity strip your real estate (or any other assets), but asset-based lenders do lend against and lien any type of property. If you have good credit, you can borrow about 80% of the value of your property from conventional lenders (banks, finance companies, etc.). "Hard-money" lenders charge higher interest, but steeper finance charges may beat losing your properties in a lawsuit.

It's easy to understand how "equity-stripping" works for asset protection. The problem is implementation. Suppose, you can't find the right lender, or you don't know the best way to encumber your assets. You can engineer a number of creative ways to structure secured loans.

We've debt-shielded the poorest credit risks. Our financing plans involved third party guarantees, or the loan proceeds collateralized "back-to-back" loans. We get loans from foreign lenders to legally and effectively encumber assets and estates worth millions. Sometimes we use complex insurance/financing arrangements – financial deals that fully encumber assets. Our financing arrangements are generally tax-neutral, and neither save nor defer taxes. For example, one car dealer in heavy litigation fully encumbered his $2 million home, vacation property, and car dealership valued at over $6 million through a complex patchwork of cross-collateralized loans. With his assets fully encumbered, we settled the 20 million dollar lawsuit against him for $100,000. Without these mortgages shielding his equity, the lawsuit would have cost him his fortune.

Equity-stripping is a vital strategy. We can arrange 95% loan/value mortgages against any type asset – real estate, a business, vehicles, notes receivable, intellectual property, and so forth. We fully encumber and creditor-proof virtually *every* U.S.-based asset. The loan proceeds are back-up collateral (secured through an offshore trust), so a strong credit rating is unnecessary. Moreover, interest on the loan is set at one-half percent *less* than what the loan proceeds earn in the offshore collateral account, so you remain cash-flow positive within the loan term. This program is likely your best equity stripping option if you have $500,000 or more in U.S.-based real estate or other assets that need protection. Debt-shielding can be simpler. Start with banks, finance companies, other conventional asset-based lenders, or family members. An affiliated company can be your "lender" if you have fewer assets to protect.

Since your spouse or close relative is considered a legally distinct party, liens or security you give these related parties is enforceable if there was fair consideration for the loan. Of course, loans from family members or affiliates make a fraudulent transfer claim more likely, and insider loans are closely scrutinized. If a court determines that your loan is a sham or without fair consideration, the court will cancel the mortgage, and your assets will be exposed to claimants.

Spouses can encumber each other's separately-owned property in "common law" states. Community property states also allow property owned and held separately to be security granted to a spouse. Loans from an affiliated business that lien your property are less likely to be upheld by the courts if you own or control the business holding the mortgage. Nevertheless, you can form a corporation, limited partnership, or LLC and give to that entity a mortgage against your property. If this mortgage is later challenged, an asset search won't reveal your relationship to that entity. A friendly lien to your own entity (one you directly or indirectly control) may, nevertheless, protect you against the less inquisitive plaintiff seeking unencumbered assets.

Aggressive asset protection specialists creatively plan to reduce the visibility of their clients' relationship to the lender entity. If you own only a minority share in the lender business and don't control the corporation or LLC, the lien is more likely to survive challenge.

Again, you need professional guidance. The more complex case may need several levels of customized foreign trusts, corporations, LLCs, private foundations or other entities. Each entity, in its own way, provides another layer of privacy, anonymity, and protection. Foreign entities are sometimes mere shells, IBCs or LLCs, with neither shareholders nor capital. Only intense investigation will enable a creditor to distinguish a shell entity from an actual operating foreign entity. A foreign shell entity may then be a reasonably good way to encumber your property. But your foreign entity must be prepared to defend its mortgage before a U.S. judge who may need to decide priorities between competing lien holders or judgment creditors.

Success with these arrangements lies in the absolute privacy available from offshore financial centers that deny plaintiff's attorneys access to their records. The complexities of multi-layer foreign entities completely severs the relationships between the U.S. property owner and the foreign IBC or LLC holding the lien against this property. But a word of caution: These transactions aren't intended to save or defer U.S. taxes. Comply with IRS offshore reporting requirements. A fully tax-compliant plan can still give you privacy and protection against litigants.

Not every debt-shield is so complex. Your "friendly liens" may simply be a mortgage to a relative, friend, or favored creditor to whom you owe money. What's important is that if your lien is later challenged, you can prove that you owe the money and that the lien isn't a sham. Anything less is illusive protection.

CREATE AN
OBLIGATION-BASED LIEN

"Cash" loans effectively equity-strip property, but they have their drawbacks. Your lender pays taxes on your interest payments, and you won't be able to fully encumber your assets through standard commercial lenders. You must also pay interest, or you may not have the credit, collateral or resources to fully equity-strip your property.

But obligations aside from cash loans can justify the lien. Liens secure a variety of obligations in the normal course of business. These executory obligations are as valid as cash loans. In fact, a lien securing an executory obligation is sometimes better than a lien securing a cash loan because there are generally no negative tax or economic consequence to fulfilling the obligation. You can also arrange for the lien not to be reduced until you fulfill your obligation. The lien amount can even grow until the obligation is fulfilled. You have no loan proceeds to protect, nor will cash shortages affect your ability to fulfill nonmonetary obligations. You also need not worry about how to get $500,000 to equity-strip your $500,000 home or office building. Cash loans are easily quantified. You can't use a large lien to secure a small loan. However, executory obligations are difficult to quantify. You can easily match the obligation to the value of the encumbered property.

As with any strategy, there are alternate ways to achieve a specific objective or goal. Can your lien secure an existing loan? Can you give a lien to secure a contract, such as a lease, or subscription to buy an interest in another entity? What other obligations can you collateralize? What future or contingent liabilities might you secure? How can you interpose "friendly" liens to shield the equity in your property? Whatever the mechanics, your goal is to leave no equity exposed or unencumbered.

DEPRESS YOUR PROPERTY'S VALUE

Homestead laws and encumbrances decrease your real estate's exposed equity. Another way to effectively lower the exposed equity is to reduce the value of your property.

What is your building worth? This largely depends on its rental income. If your building is occupied by only your business, a long-term, low rent lease between your real estate entity and your business depresses the value of the real estate to a creditor seeking to seize the property. Your property is even less attractive if the low rent creates a negative cash flow for a new property owner. Further depress the value of your property. Assign the rents to a more friendly creditor through an assignment of lease as collateral security for obligations due that secured creditor. You see the concept.

Another tactic: give a friendly third party an option to buy your real estate. The option may be for 75-80% of value. An option to buy property – provided the price is reasonable – will withstand creditor challenge. A creditor who then seizes the optioned property takes it subject to the recorded option. The creditor cannot sell the property while the option is enforceable. Again, the property is thus less valuable to the creditor.

There are a number of devaluation methods. For example, a property may pass through a number of sales – each transfer for a price 5-10% less than the preceding sale. This successive "discounting" is more likely to avoid fraudulent transfer claims than will a single transaction where the property is sold at too great a discount.

INDIRECTLY MANAGE YOUR PROPERTY

It isn't enough to protect your interest in your real estate.

Real estate, particularly investment and rental properties, creates enormous liabilities ranging from breach of lease, to "slip and fall," to environmental and toxic waste claims. This is another reason to title your commercial properties to an LLC. The manager generally has no personal responsibility for the debts of the LLC. Nevertheless, the LLC should carry adequate liability insurance. It's also wise to form another LLC or corporation to manage the LLC that owns the property. This further distances you personally from potential personal liability.

In sum, shield yourself from "outside-in" and "inside-out" liability. "Outside-in" means that your ownership of the property cannot be claimed by your personal creditors. "Inside-out" insulates you and your personal assets from liabilities arising from your owning or managing the property.

CHAPTER 4

FINANCIAL SELF-DEFENSE FOR YOUR INVESTMENTS

What can we do to shield your cash, mutual funds, annuities, stocks, bonds, CD's and other liquid investments? Set aside for the moment your retirement accounts. We'll cover them in the next chapter.

Are your liquid assets now safe? How are they titled? How can you better fortify them?

You have several options. Which is best for you will depend upon your personal situation, the value of these assets, your estate plan, and your financial and tax objectives. Involve your financial planner, tax advisor and insurance professional in your planning, so you not only protect these assets, but also structure them correctly considering your other goals. Your financial professionals are integral members of your wealth protection team. They are essential to a coordinated, integrated plan.

TRANSFER YOUR INVESTMENTS
TO A LIMITED PARTNERSHIP

We usually use the limited partnership to protect our clients' liquid investments. If you are the general partner, you'll completely control these assets. You indirectly own these same assets as a limited partner. Limited partnership assets are well-protected and beyond the reach of future creditor claims. Limited partnerships are tax-neutral, reversible and easily maintained. They have virtually no disadvantages.

Most asset protection attorneys agree that the limited partnership (and LLC) are the two entities that can most advantageously protect liquid assets – particularly domestic (U.S.-based) investments.

The limited partnership protects investment assets in the same way the LLC protects real estate. Creditors of a limited or general partner cannot seize their limited partnership interest. The judgment creditor's remedy is a charging order against the debtor's limited partnership interest. This charging order gives the creditor only the right to claim profits and liquidation proceeds payable to the limited partner. The charging order doesn't give the creditor the rights of a substitute partner, nor does the creditor gain other partnership rights. The creditor cannot sell, auction or foreclose upon the partnership interest, nor vote, nor inspect partnership books. The creditor becomes only a mere assignee of the limited partner for purposes of collecting profits or distributions once voted by the general partners and distributed to the debtor limited partner.

The rationale behind the charging order is to protect the other partners uninvolved in the debts of the debtor-partner from undue interference in partnership affairs by that debtor-partner's creditors. A corporate shareholder's creditors can foreclose upon the debtor-shareholder's shares. Whoever buys these shares becomes a full successor stockholder with every stockholder right. This distinction is what makes the limited partnership (or LLC) so advantageous.

Your limited partnership can protect numerous assets: cash, investment securities, notes, receivables, investment real estate, patents, trademarks, copyrights, shares in a C corporation, and LLC membership interests. In exchange for the transfer of your personal assets to your LP, you receive your partnership interest. Your asset contributions can also be loans to the limited partnership, however this gives you less protection because your creditor can claim the future re-payments due you from the LP.

Your limited partnership should own only assets suitable for business or investment purposes. LPs are income-producing entities. Generally, your LP shouldn't own your family residence because you'd lose the tax advantages from personal home ownership. Collectibles, jewelry, coins, artwork and antiques are appropriate for an LP if you expect them to increase in value. An LP cannot own shares in an S corporation, but can own C corporation shares as well as LLC memberships. Your IRA and other retirement accounts shouldn't be owned by your LP. Annuities can be owned by an LP, but you may lose their tax deferral benefits. Check this out with your accountant. Don't title autos, boats or other vehicles to an LP unless they are used to operate the LP. Keep liability-producing assets out of your LP.

As we said in the last chapter, have your real estate owned by a limited liability company (LLC), and not an LP, because real estate, like autos and boats, are liability-producing assets and can create lawsuits and personal liability for the general partners.

Having a corporation or LLC as the general partner limits this liability, but the better alternative is to use an LLC to hold liability-producing assets, and the limited partnership to hold "safe" (non-liability producing) assets.

DEFENSIVELY STRUCTURE
YOUR LIMITED PARTNERSHIP

Limited partners can allocate their ownership interests or profit distributions as they elect. This is important for protection. For instance, you can contribute personal assets to the partnership for a proportionately smaller partnership share. The remaining limited partnership interest can be owned by other family members. However, you make a taxable gift if the other family members are other than your spouse. Have your accountant review your limited partnership proposed structure to avoid tax liability. Also have your accountant determine that the LP is a favorable entity from a tax standpoint.

Families adopt typical limited partnership structures. For example, mom and dad may form the LP and contribute various income-producing investments in exchange for their partnership interests. As general partners, they each receive a two percent partnership interest. As general partners, they equally control the partnership, as they jointly controlled the contributed assets. As limited partners, mom and dad receive the remaining 96% limited partnership interest. (General and limited partners can be the same parties). Mom and dad now exclusively and equally own and control the partnership and its assets. There's no real change from when their assets were titled to their individual names – only now their assets are protected.

Other structures are possibilities. If dad has creditors, mom may become the sole general partner. Or mom and dad could form a corporation or LLC as the general partner. This is a particularly good arrangement if the partnership can incur liabilities for which the general partners would have liability. A corporation or LLC as the general partner also adds more privacy as to who personally is involved in the entity.

You can easily modify limited partnership structures. Mom may eventually own a greater interest, or parents may gradually gift their limited partnership interests to their children, to a living trust, or to another entity. The limited partnership's flexible structure works especially well for estate planning and lifetime gifting.

BOLSTER YOUR
LIMITED PARTNERSHIP PROTECTION

As with the LLC, your protection with a limited partnership largely depends on you having the most protective provisions in your agreement. These "bulletproofing" clauses are similar to those used to bolster LLC protection.

1. Your limited partnership agreement should give the general partners full and absolute discretion to make or withhold profit distributions.

2. Your agreement should prohibit transfers of limited partnership interests without the consent of the general partner and/or a majority – or even of a unanimous number of the other limited partners.

3. Your agreement should prevent a limited partner from withdrawing their capital contributions without unanimous partner consent.

4. Specify in the agreement that a creditor of a limited partner becomes only an assignee of the limited partner's interest and acquires no partnership rights other than rights to distributions.

5. The partnership agreement should give the general partner the right to "assess" the limited partners for contributions, and extend this assessment to charging order creditors. This anti-creditor strategy is particularly effective.

6. Allocate "high-risk" family members fewer partnership profits. Allocate more profits to "low-risk" family members.

7. Give your limited partnership an "option to purchase" or redeem a bankrupt or debtor partner's partnership interest.

8. Spouses in a tenancy-by-the-entirety state might title their limited partnership interests as tenants-by-the-entirety, which further protects their limited partnership interest against one spouse's creditors.

9. If you invest in a limited partnership or limited liability company that you don't control, title your ownership interest to a family limited partnership that you do control. This protects your distributions from the non-controlled entity.

Finally, consider where to set up your limited partnership. Limited partnership laws follow the Uniform Limited Partnership Law (ULPA); however, some states have stronger LP laws. For example, California is the least friendly to limited partnerships. In several cases, California courts permitted a partner's creditors seize and sell a debtor-partner's partnership interest. Florida is more debtor-friendly. It specifically limits, by statute, the creditor remedy to the charging order. Are your state laws sufficiently strong? That question is for your lawyer.

USE AN OFFSHORE TRUST AS
THE LIMITED PARTNER

For maximum protection, set up an offshore asset protection trust as the limited partner. You, and/or other family members, can be the general partners and control the partnership. If there's a serious threat to the partnership assets, the partnership can liquidate and distribute its assets to the limited partner – the offshore trust. Partnership assets offshore will have considerably more protection. Moreover, if an offshore trust owns the limited partnership interest, a charging order against you would be ineffective against the trust.

A limited partnership gives you considerably greater protection than titling assets to yourself individually. But it still gives far less protection than an offshore trust or another protective foreign structure that places your assets beyond the reach of U.S. courts and claimants. You can physically transfer liquid assets offshore. You have a different problem with U.S.-based assets, such as real estate. The limited partnership (or LLC) gives you less than absolute protection here because these assets are physically within the United States and remain subject to U.S. court jurisdiction. Faced with a serious lawsuit, your strategy is to sell or encumber your U.S.-based assets and then transfer the proceeds, first to a limited partnership, and then to an offshore trust as its limited partner.

SEND YOUR TAX BILL TO
AN UNWARY CREDITOR

Smart creditors don't ask for a charging order against a debtor-partner of a limited partnership (or LLC). The creditor won't collect if there's no distribution. However, the creditor might get a huge income tax bill.

Interestingly, IRS rules make a charging order creditor liable for income taxes on partnership income attributable to the debtor partner. For instance, if the partnership earns $100,000 and the debtor partner owns half the partnership, that debtor partner has $50,000 taxable income, regardless of whether the partner received these profits. This is "phantom" or "pass through" income. Generally, the charging order creditor instead becomes liable for the tax on the debtor partner's $50,000 income attribution even if the creditor received no partnership profits under the charging order. The prospect of a tax bill, rather than payment, discourages all but the most foolhardy creditor from obtaining a charging order against a limited partnership (or LLC) interest.

DON'T MAKE FRAUDULENT TRANSFERS TO YOUR LIMITED PARTNERSHIP

Here's a common mistake with LPs (and LLCs): You are sued. To protect your assets you transfer them to an LP for a disproportionately small (or no) partnership interest because you don't want your creditor to pursue your LP interest with a charging order.

Your objective is logical, but it can be a fatal way to structure your LP. You want to exchange your personal assets for a partnership interest that is proportionate to your invested asset; otherwise your present creditor can recover the transferred assets as a fraudulent transfer. Your partnership interest's value approximates the value of your contributed assets, or it would be a fraudulent conveyance.

Still, some courts set aside transfers to an LP (or LLC) against a *present* creditor – even when the debtor assets were exchanged for a proportionate partnership or LLC interest. That's why you may need *more* protection than you can get through an LP or LLC – if you have a *present* creditor. As before, the answer is to liquidate or encumber your assets and transfer the proceeds; first into the limited partnership or LLC, and then into the offshore asset protection trust.

CUT YOUR ESTATE TAXES WITH YOUR LP

Estate planners love limited partnerships too. LPs do more than protect savings and possessions from lawsuits and creditors. LPs also reduce estate taxes. An LP might save your family thousands, or millions. Here's how: Your estate pays taxes on what you own at death, so a common tax-saving strategy is to gift your assets over your lifetime to your intended beneficiaries. When you die, the government has fewer assets to tax. But lifetime gifting has its drawbacks; you lose control over the gifted property. But if your LP owns the asset(s), you can gift your LP interests to your beneficiaries. As the general partner you control the assets during your lifetime. You can bequeath to your family, or other beneficiaries, more wealth because your estate pays less estate taxes on a smaller estate.

You may not want to gift your LP partnership interests within your lifetime. You'll then die owning your entire LP interest, subject to estate tax. You'll still pay the IRS less. Your limited partnership interest value won't be your percentage ownership in the LP times the fair market value of the LP assets as you might expect. It's less. LP interests are valued at a discount. The IRS considers an LP interest, which owns an asset, to be worth less than the same asset owned outright. The IRS allows a *lack of marketability* discount because your LP interest isn't readily marketable. What market is there for an LP interest when the other partners are family members? If you die owning less than 50% of the LP, the IRS further allows you a *minority ownership* discount. There's also little market for LP interests controlled by others. In sum, *the IRS values your LP interest 15% to 40% less than your percentage fair market value share.* You can save thousands or millions if you have a larger estate.

GO OFFSHORE
WITH YOUR MONEY

Protect as much of your wealth offshore as possible.

Protecting wealth in foreign lands has been popular for wealthy families since Roman emperors preserved their riches in foreign territories. So did the Crusaders. Offshore asset protection is no less important for Americans; and never more necessary than today because of our litigation explosion. Foreign trusts and other protective, debtor-friendly entities and laws featured by offshore financial centers have given planners a vital new tool for wealth preservation. *Trillions* are now protected in foreign trusts in *offshore financial centers,* whose favorable banking, privacy, estate planning and asset protection laws make these countries attractive places to shield one's money. Wealthy individuals and families internationally have trusts in protective countries, and have for decades. Only within the past decade or two, have American professionals, entrepreneurs and businesspeople taken advantage of these same foreign wealth-preservation opportunities.

Unfortunately, too *few* Americans have offshore protection. Some think that stockpiling money in a foreign trust is illegal, that only drug dealers, money launderers or tax evaders do it. They're wrong. Offshore trusts and other foreign entities are perfectly legal. It's also a great way to protect your hard-earned wealth.

A foreign asset protection trust (FAPT), or any other offshore entity, *won't save you U.S. taxes*. A FAPT has no tax consequences. It won't help or hurt you tax-wise. The FAPT's sole purpose is to protect your wealth against future threats – as well as give you a vehicle for offshore investing. Pay your taxes on your offshore earnings, and follow IRS reporting requirements. You'll stay trouble-free.

How does the FAPT protect assets? Begin with the concept of *jurisdiction*. American courts have jurisdiction only over persons or property within the U.S., not individuals or property in other countries. If your FAPT is in one of the offshore financial centers that doesn't recognize foreign judgments, your creditor must sue the trust in that foreign country's courts. That's usually impractical, if not impossible. Consider the obstacles. The trustee holding legal title to the trust assets is outside the U.S. (foreign trustee companies without U.S. ties), so a U.S. court cannot order the trustee to turn over the trust assets to your claimant. U.S. courts have no jurisdiction over the foreign trustee and also no jurisdiction over the foreign assets. Assets *within* the U.S. are different. A U.S. court could order these assets (real estate, local bank accounts, stocks of U.S. corporations, and so forth) transferred to your creditor.

That's why, when you're seriously threatened, you want to move your vulnerable wealth offshore. American courts with jurisdiction over neither the trustee nor the trust assets are powerless to recover your assets. With the American courts powerless to recover assets from your FAPT, a claimant seeking assets from your FAPT must file suit in the offshore financial center. This is an extraordinarily time-consuming, expensive and usually fruitless proposition. These countries are extremely debtor-protective. Few American creditors ever recover assets from offshore trusts.

The FAPT's formidable protection encourages small settlements. Most plaintiffs settle cheaply once they discover the defendant's wealth is sheltered in a FAPT. Shielding wealth offshore is the best way to encourage settlement or discourage a lawsuit. Few contingency lawyers accept a case when they are to be paid from assets they must recover from a FAPT. It's usually a losing proposition.

No asset protection plan is 100% creditor-proof. Offshore asset protection, as with any domestic plan, works only if done correctly. There are rules to follow. Transfer your assets offshore *before* you have a creditor. Give control of the offshore assets to the foreign trustee. Have the proper documents. Select trustees to whom you can safely entrust your assets. Several offshore trusts have failed, and debtors have been jailed for contempt because they ignored one or more of these warnings. Offshore asset protection is complex. You'll need an experienced attorney to avoid the pitfalls. Still, nearly every asset protection attorney agrees that transferring your money offshore is your safest financial self-defense strategy.

ALTERNATIVELY, SET UP A FOREIGN LLC

The foreign Limited Liability Company is sometimes a good alternative to the FAPT.

Every state and many foreign jurisdictions have LLCs. Nevis (in the West Indies) LLCs are particularly popular for asset protection because of its many unique features. The Nevis

LLC can be member-directed or managed by a foreign director. For protection, have your LLC controlled by a foreign (Nevis) managing director. This transfer of control protects LLC assets from U.S. court orders. A judgment creditor can only get a charging order against your Nevis LLC. As with U.S.-based LLCs, the charging order gives the creditor only the right to collect distributions payable to you from the LLC. Your LLC interest cannot itself be seized, nor can your creditor vote your interest, or exercise any other member rights, such as inspecting LLC books and records and so forth. Nevis law also imposes U.S. income tax liability to the charging order creditor for the debtor-member's apportioned profits-even if the creditor receives no distributions. These same protective features are found with U.S. limited partnerships and LLCs, but not with other protective offshore entities. A Nevis LLC also delegates all power to the managing director who, like a trustee of an offshore trust, would ignore U.S. court repatriation orders. If the LLC has at least two members, as it should, the operating agreement would require unanimous member vote to change the managing director. This stifles a court order compelling one debtor member to replace the director. The Nevis LLC then, conceptually, protects assets in much the same manner as an offshore trust, except that the debtor member may own the LLC and derivatively, its assets.

You "gift" assets to the trust. You make a *qui pro quo* transfer of assets for the LLC interest. If you have a present creditor, under Nevis LLC law you can transfer your assets to the LLC and it's *not* considered a fraudulent conveyance, provided your membership interest is proportionate to your contributed capital. Interestingly, Nevis law lets a promised future capital contribution by other LLC members to be used to measure this proportionality. You then have the flexibility to advantageously apportion your LLC membership interests. In several respects, the Nevis LLC is more protective than a foreign trust or domestic limited partnership. Regardless of your financial situation, you can use the Nevis LLC without fear of a fraudulent transfer claim.

The Cook Islands is another favorite asset protection jurisdiction. It has recently enacted LLC legislation. Their LLCs are about as protective as the Nevis LLC, but the Cook Islands have a shorter statute of limitations. We use both Nevis and Cook Island LLCs.

As with the offshore trust, the foreign LLC is tax-neutral. A U.S. taxpayer pays taxes on the LLC's earnings in the year earned, not when the earnings are repatriated. IRS reporting requirements for LLCs are less burdensome than for offshore trusts, and LLC's administrative and set up costs are also less.

When should you use a foreign trust, and when an LLC? The answer depends on many factors. You can invest internationally through either entity. You also gain excellent creditor protection from either. The foreign trust lets you do estate planning, yet it won't save you estate taxes. But to protect smaller estates, the foreign LLC may be your answer, if only because it's less costly.

MULTIPLY YOUR OFFSHORE ENTITIES

When you have a lot of money offshore (say, over $500,000), use separate structures with different trustees in different financial centers.

Diversity = protection. It's far more difficult for a creditor to seize assets in multiple entities and jurisdictions. The downside: multiple entities cost more to set up and maintain. How many eggs do you want in any one basket? What's it worth to have more baskets?

Numerous diversification possibilities exist. For instance, your Cook Island trust (FAPT) can own a Nevis LLC. A Panamanian foundation may own a Panamanian IBC. For geographic diversification, split your assets between a Cook Island trust and a Nevis trust, using different trustee firms. You see the idea.

Several jurisdictions give excellent asset protection. Nevis and the Cook Island are favorites, but the Isle of Man, Belize, Turks and Caicos, Panama, Gibralter and Malta are good. We don't recommend the Bahamas, Caymans or Switzerland.

Also choose from a range of protective entities. The FAPT and foreign LLC are most common, but other jurisdictions have foundations, hybrid companies, companies limited by guarantee, limited partnerships and IBCs. Each entity can be part of a diversified plan.

"Daisy-chain" or multi-entity arrangements don't change your tax responsibilities. No matter your structure, report and pay taxes on your offshore earnings annually. Nor is it about hiding your money. Honestly disclose your assets when under oath. Your only purpose is to impose more procedural obstacles, enough to overwhelm a creditor. Layered, diversified offshore plans present an insurmountable obstacle that can dissuade *any* creditor.

UPGRADE YOUR PROTECTION, FORGET FOREIGN CORPORATIONS

An IBC (foreign corporation) can *privatize* offshore wealth. But, privacy isn't protection. A creditor who discovers your money in an offshore company (IBC) can have an American court order you to transfer your IBC ownership to your creditor. The court can also order you to liquidate your IBC and return its assets to your creditor. Nor will courts believe that money mysteriously "disappeared" into the bowels of a foreign company. For protection, you need a protective structure. An IBC isn't that entity. Offshore IBC promoters "sell" protection as one of its benefits, but don't be misled. You need a FAPT and/or a foreign LLC to protect you. An IBC can be a subsidiary of an offshore trust (the IBC becomes the investment subsidiary for the parent trust) but it's smarter to use a Nevis or Cook Island LLC as the trust subsidiary. The LLC's protective features are greater than an IBC's.

Bank accounts in your name in a privacy haven also need protection. Your account must also be reported on your tax returns (you must report annually to the Treasury). A court can order you to repatriate money in the account since you control the account (remember, you don't control a FAPT or foreign LLC.)

Offshore banking records are protected against U.S. court orders and subpoenas, so offshore banks in the better privacy countries are jurisdictionally immune to process. These offshore banks also ban U.S. writs of execution or attachment orders. In that sense, their secrecy laws somewhat protect entrusted funds from creditor seizure. If your offshore bank has no American-based branch or affiliate, you gain limited protection against a creditor claim, but the offshore bank account titled to you personally is still poorly protected.

USE A CAPTIVE INSURANCE COMPANY (CIC) FOR PROTECTION AND TAX SAVINGS

Whenever we speak on tax-efficient wealth planning, we are asked about offshore captive insurance companies (CIC's). "Captives" give you protection if they're set up and maintained properly. But they must meet your business and insurance needs. They must make financial sense for you.

The CIC is an offshore insurance company licensed to write insurance within the U.S. and registered with the IRS. "Captives" are typically based in Bermuda or the British Virgin Islands, which require small capitalization and have good insurance and tax laws. They write about one-third of the commercial insurance sold in the United States. Fortune 500 companies use CIC's to protect their assets and for tax benefits. Within the past decade many small business owners and professionals have followed.

A CIC can insure all or some of your business or professional practice's risks, such as malpractice. You can, however, insure yourself against any high liability, non-malpractice risk; wrongful termination; sexual harassment or any other possible liability for which you might not be able to buy insurance. When you self-insure against these "uninsurable" risks, you pay these claims from "after tax" dollars. Conversely, you take current year tax deductions and pay claims with *pre-tax* dollars from CICs loss reserves. The CIC can also insure low liability risks. In addition, your CIC can also transfer risks to other reinsurers, so there's less economic risk to your CIC. You still obtain the tax benefits.

More physicians and business owners "self-insure" against potential losses. Premiums paid to their CIC are fully tax deductible, while funds they would otherwise set aside to self-insure are not. Your CIC lets you fully deduct your premiums each year and protect yourself against the same risks you would "self-insure" against through set-aside programs. Self-insuring funds remain titled to your business or practice and exposed to lawsuits. On the other hand, the CIC transfers your premiums to an independent, fully-licensed insurance company offshore. These premiums are fully protected from claims against your business or practice. Should you organize a CIC? It's probably worthwhile if you're that professional or business owner who pays at least $400,000 a year for liability or casualty insurance.

BECOME MORE KNOWLEDGEABLE

Offshore wealth protection is a fascinating subject. Educate yourself! Read other books and journals about the world of offshore finance. You'll more confidently embrace offshore financial self-defense. Check other Garrett books at *www.garrettpub.com*. *How to Protect Your Money Offshore* reveals how the offshore world really works. Our forthcoming *Offshore Wealth: Secrets and Strategies for Financial Protection, Privacy and International Wealth-building* is a great resource for these troubled times.

Talk to others who have their wealth offshore. More Americans than you might expect have wealth offshore. They'll share their experiences and calm your fears. We, too, know your questions: How safe will my money be offshore? Will the trustee run away with *my* money? Will they lose my money on some crazy investment? Can I *really* get my money back when I need it? Is it legal? Does it work? Undoubtedly, these are your concerns. Others had these same concerns.

Share *their* offshore experience. You'll find their wealth safe and secure. One client comments, "I didn't realize how vulnerable my wealth was here in the U.S., until it was safely sheltered offshore." "I was nervous about moving my money offshore. Now I get anxious thinking about how easily I could have lost it here." Knowledge builds confidence and confidence prompts action.

That's why we want educated clients. It builds confidence. Learn more! Your offshore program will get underway more smoothly and enthusiastically!

BUY SELF-PROTECTED INVESTMENTS FOR YOUR PORTFOLIO

Let's investigate another approach. Federal and state exemptions help protect your cash and investments. Objective: Convert unprotected investments into exempt, creditor-protected investments. Retirement accounts are self-protected investments. We'll cover them in the next chapter. Your strategy here is to buy life insurance and/or insurance-related – products such as fixed or variable annuities – *if* these financial products are creditor-protected in your state. This takes analysis. Not every state fully protects insurance products. Many states give them no protection if you purchase them after you have a debt or claim. So timing is important.

You might liquidate your unprotected mutual funds and buy a protected variable annuity with a similar portfolio, but whether you should shift your unprotected portfolio into protected financial products depends on several *ifs*. You should, *if* you cannot protect your portfolio in any other way, *if* the products you buy are *fully* protected, and *if* these products make financial sense for you. Hundreds of financial products are self-protected, and you should consider this feature when you choose your investments. However, let your financial advisor and insurance professional help you decide whether self-protected investments would better meet your financial needs, and consider the tax consequences from liquidating your current investments.

INVEST IN A FOREIGN ANNUITY
FOR STRONGER PROTECTION

Foreign annuities can give you rock-solid protection. State laws usually exempt annuities from creditor seizure. Yet even if it's protected, you'll get far stronger protection if you buy an Isle of Man or Swiss annuity (several other countries also offer creditor-protected annuities). Foreign annuities also provide other important financial advantages over a U.S. annuity. Check the tax consequences if you do buy a foreign annuity. They aren't all tax-deferred. And buy your foreign annuity through an offshore trust or foreign LLC. This further insulates your annuity from creditor claims. If your state creditor-protects annuities, you then have *triple* protection: 1) your state laws, 2) the protective entity (that owns the annuity), and 3) exemption protection from the Isle of Man or Switzerland.

You can purchase foreign annuities from triple A-rated foreign companies. They'll give you precisely the portfolio that's right for you, selecting from a wide range of international investments. You can also trade in different currencies and gain an edge over the declining U.S. dollar. The Isle of Man gives near-absolute protection to its annuities, and, as of this writing, is the jurisdiction of choice. For more information, visit *www. AssetProtectionAttorneys.com*.

OPEN AN OUT-OF-STATE
BANK ACCOUNT

Put your serious money offshore. And deposit your domestic money in another state. Your creditor must then get a judgment from that state before seizing your out-of-state funds. Courts in your state cannot order the seizure of your property in another state. That's why it can be even wiser to deploy your assets in several states. It's a perfectly legal tactic to frustrate creditor collection. For more protection, don't title your bank account to your personal name. Set up an LLC or limited partnership in that state. Of course, money in another state isn't nearly as protected as money offshore because your creditor can get a judgment in that state. But it's still a small hurdle for your creditor.

Let's warn you about another classic mistake. Never keep your bank accounts or investments in any bank to which you owe money. Your lenders can, without notice, apply these funds to your loan. Keep your money only in banks where you have *no* obligations.

PREPAY EXPENSES WITH EXPOSED CASH

Perhaps you don't have much money to protect. How can you legally dispose of your money if you're in financial trouble? Which creditors should you pay? What debts that are non-dischargeable in bankruptcy, can you pay? Which creditors – family, friends or favored creditors – can you pay (watch preferences if you plan bankruptcy). What future expenses can you prepay? Car payments, rents, tuitions, insurance premiums or even paying the IRS for *future* obligations are all possibilities.

**CREDITOR-PROOF
YOUR BUSINESS OWNERSHIP**

Your LLC and limited partnership give you "charging order-only protection," but corporate shares can be seized by a judgment creditor or bankruptcy trustee. You'd then lose ownership in your corporation. So whether you own a family business or a tiny slice of a Fortune 500 company, protectively title whatever corporate shares you own individually or together with your spouse.

- Married? Transfer most, or all, of the corporate shares to the less vulnerable spouse. You'll no longer control the corporation, so make certain this meets your personal, estate planning and divorce-proofing objectives.

- Title shares in a "C" corporation (not an "S" corporation) to a family limited partnership (FLP). As the general partner you'd control the partnership assets. You and/or your spouse may be the general partners, and you, and/or your spouse, children, or trusts may be limited partners.

- Transfer your corporate shares to an irrevocable trust for your children or other beneficiaries. For example, you and/or your spouse may be the co-trustees and manage the trust that controls the corporate shares. As trustees, you indirectly control the corporate assets.

- Title your shares to an LLC. As with a limited partnership, a member's personal creditor cannot seize the LLC membership interest. But watch the fraudulent transfer laws if you have creditors.

- Title your C corporation shares to an offshore trust. Offshore trusts well-protect corporate shares. Or use an offshore trust as the limited partner of an LP, which would become the corporate shareholder. This greatly strengthens your protection.

- Title C or S corporation shares as tenants-by-the-entirety if you co-own the shares with your spouse, and if your state protects corporate shares co-owned as tenancy-by-the-entirety.

It's more difficult to protect S corporation shares. S corporation shares cannot be owned by other entities (other than single member LLCs and special offshore trusts). But you might convert your S corporation to an LLC or C corporation. Discuss this with your accountant and attorney. Your S corporation shares can also be owned by a single member LLC or a special type offshore trust. Finally, you can pledge your S corporation shares as security.

Some debtors camouflage their corporate ownership. That's usually a poor tactic. Diligent creditors identify corporate shareholders through corporate books, tax returns, licensing applications, public records and so forth. Still, a foreign corporation from an offshore financial center might own your U.S. company. Your lawyer and accountant can guide you on the tax and reporting requirements involving your foreign corporate ownership. Stay less visible. Don't be a corporate officer or director. Officers or directors of closely-owned corporations are assumed to own some financial interest in the business.

COLLATERIZE YOUR INVESTMENTS

Equity-stripping or debt shields can protect your home and other real estate. It works as well for other investments. Pledge your investments as primary or secondary collateral to secure loans. One danger: don't give a lender too much collateral. This may not work to your advantage. But it might make sense if you have a "friendlier" lender.

Creatively "bundle" as collateral your hard assets (real estate, equipment, vehicles, etc.) and liquid assets (CDs, stocks, bonds, etc.) so that these assets are all protected under one loan. There are any number of ways to structure this. Our loan programs encumber 95% of value of U.S. liquid assets (stocks, bonds, interests in family businesses, etc.). These assets can remain in their present form in the U.S. It's not necessary to liquidate your portfolio to encumber and make your portfolio worthless to creditors.

MULTIPLY YOUR INVESTMENTS PROTECTION

Chapter 2 explains why and how to layer your plan to multiply your protection. We combine firewalls – homestead laws, LLCs and mortgages or debt-shields to shelter your home and real estate. You could also multiply the protection for your other investments. Will a creditor attempt to pursue assets that you transferred to: 1) a limited partnership, 2) then, to an offshore trust, 3) then, to a foreign LLC, and 4) finally, to a self-protected foreign annuity? Those four formidable protective layers are a daunting challenge to any creditor. Add more protection. Secure the annuities as collateral for an offshore loan program. Voila! You have five layers insulating your nest egg. These multiple steps are what you need when you have a sizeable portfolio or a determined creditor and want bulletproof wealth!

CHAPTER 5

FINANCIAL SELF-DEFENSE

FOR YOUR RETIREMENT ACCOUNTS

Retirement! What's more sacred than your "nest egg"? It's your pension or IRA account that will see you through your golden years. Sadly, you may have already lost much of your nest egg to bad investments, failed pension programs or the economy. Your 401(k) is a 201(k) or a 101(k). But there's still other predatory dangers – the challenges this book is about. How can you be sure *any* of your nest egg will still be there when it's time to stop punching the clock?

DON'T ASSUME YOUR RETIREMENT PLAN IS PROTECTED

Is your retirement plan lawsuit-proof? You might think so, but you could be wrong. Not every retirement plan is. For protection purposes, we can divide retirement plans into: 1) ERISA-qualified plans, and 2) non-qualified retirement plans (such as Individual Retirement Accounts).

ERISA-qualified plans come under the Employee Retirement Income Security Act of 1974 (ERISA). This law protects employees in benefit plans sponsored by their employers or unions. One ERISA requirement is that ERISA pension plans include a spendthrift trust that prohibits the beneficiary (or the beneficiary's creditors) from gifting, anticipating, claiming or encumbering the plan's principal or income. Common ERISA qualified retirement plans are profit-sharing plans (defined contribution plans), pension plans (defined benefit plans), and 401(k) plans where the employee makes voluntary contributions to their plan. In sum, ERISA-qualified plans cannot be claimed by creditors, whether in bankruptcy or through lawsuits. *All* ERISA-qualified pension and profit-sharing plans are *usually* protected. Public pensions (funded by state or federal governments) have always been creditor protected. Still, ERISA protection isn't absolute. It can, in certain circumstances, be illusory.

An ERISA-qualified plan isn't safe from every creditor. ERISA plans aren't the holy grail of asset protection in all instances. Although the ERISA's anti-alienation clause provides strong protection against private creditors, other statutes make it clear ERISA-governed plans are unprotected against:

- Federal tax claims.
- Federal criminal fines and restitution orders.

- Child support payments, alimony payments, or forfeiture/division of the plan due to divorce.

- A criminal or civil judgment, consent order, decree, or settlement arising from a plan participant's fiduciary violation or crime against the plan. (In this situation, only the offending party's portion of the plan is forfeited.)

These foregoing claims may lead to attachment of ERISA-governed pensions, notwithstanding ERISA's anti-alienation provision.

Nor is every pension plan ERISA-qualified. For example, one ERISA requirement is that in addition to the company owners, at least one non-family employee be a plan beneficiary. Other technical requirements must also be observed. Violating any one rule can cause the plan to lose ERISA protection. If you are uncertain whether your plan is fully ERISA-qualified and compliant, have your lawyer or plan administrator review your pension documents.

The technical and tax compliance requirements to maintain an ERISA-qualified plan are considerable. One presumes that larger companies plans are ERISA qualified, but that's less true for the smaller firm whose plans inadvertently and oftentimes lose ERISA status. Its beneficiaries then lose creditor protection. Several recent cases have shown this protection erosion for retirement accounts. In these cases, claimants successfully argued that the debtor's 401(k) plans didn't fully comply with IRS/ERISA regulations and, therefore, their plan was not entitled to ERISA protection. These plans then had only whatever protection was available to non-qualified plans under the debtor's state laws.

Multiple participant Keogh plans are lawsuit protected to the same extent as ERISA-qualified pensions. But sole participant

Keogh plans are not. In most states, IRAs are less protected than ERISA-qualified plans and Keoghs, which enjoy federal protection. IRAs have no spendthrift provisions, trustees, or federal protection, other than in bankruptcy. Non-qualified ERISA plans include Simplified Employee Pension (SEP) accounts, Roth IRAs, single-owner ERISA qualified plans and IRAs.

Is a non-qualified plan protected in your state against lawsuits and creditors? There's no blanket federal lawsuit immunity as with ERISA-qualified plans. Protection for the non-qualified plan depends solely upon state law, except for the debtor in bankruptcy. As with other state exemptions (homestead, insurance, wages, etc.), state laws vary. Some states fully protect non-qualified accounts. Others give little or no lawsuit protection to non-qualified plans. Most states partially protect non-qualified plans. Their statutory protection may be for a fixed amount (i.e., $50,000) of for whatever amount a court considers reasonably necessary for the debtor's retirement. You'll find other limitations or restrictions under your state statutes.

Some states protect accounts in trust, but not distributions made to a beneficiary. Nor are Roth IRAs necessarily as protected as IRAs. Several states have yet to amend their laws to extend IRA statutory protection to Roths. You can experience this same problem with SEP-IRAs. One conclusion from all this: every ERISA qualified pension plan, and *every* IRA and other non-qualified plan must be carefully reviewed by your asset protection or bankruptcy lawyer. Don't *assume* your plan is protected. You could be wrong! You'll then need the strategies in this chapter to shelter your *unprotected* retirement plan.

**DON'T QUICKLY
ROLLOVER YOUR 401(K)**

Hesitate before you rollover your pension into a self-directed IRA. Consider the protection you might lose. Rollovers of ERISA-qualified pensions into a self-directed IRA that your state doesn't fully protect reduces or eliminates your creditor protection. You may not have the option to leave your retirement account in your employer's 401(k) plan, or you may want to self-direct your investments through an IRA. The rollover decision should primarily be an investment decision. But consider asset protection as an important factor before you do a rollover. If you can keep your money in your pension plan and if you're satisfied with the pension's investment performance, it's certainly safer to have a fully sheltered pension rather than a partially or completely unprotected IRA.

If it's smart to lawsuit-proof your retirement funds by keeping it in an ERISA-qualified plan, it can be as wise to rollback your IRA into an ERISA-qualified plan, provided your IRA was originally a rollover from an ERISA-qualified plan. Or create your own ERISA qualified plan. A number of zero-percent money purchase plans are IRS compliant, ERISA-qualified, and creditor-proof. Similarly, if your pension plan isn't fully protected (such as a single member plan) then add one or more non-family beneficiaries to create a creditor-protected ERISA.

RELOCATE TO A STATE
THAT FULLY PROTECTS IRAs

Extreme cases demand extreme measures. Is moving your answer?

If you have a large, unprotected IRA and big legal or financial problems (and if it's practical), relocate to a state that fully protects IRAs. This is essentially the same strategy as homestead "shopping." You move to the most protective jurisdiction to shelter your home. No, it's not insane if you have mobility or a huge IRA and bankruptcy is not a good option for you. Also physically relocate your IRA to your new state so it comes under your state's protective laws. You'll lose your state protection if your IRA stays in a less-protective state. Also reside in your new state for the required time to claim its IRA exemption.

SHELTER EXTRA CASH INTO YOUR
PROTECTED RETIREMENT ACCOUNT

Here's another interesting possibility. Use your retirement plan as your safe haven for your extra cash. It can be sensible if your retirement plan is fully creditor-protected. Yes, you have limits on how much you can put into your retirement plan on a *tax deferred basis,* but you *can* invest more *after-tax* dollars into a lawsuit-proof retirement plan. Once you reach the tax-deferred annual contribution to your retirement plan, pay the tax on the excess contributions. It will nevertheless be protected by your plan.

**INVEST YOUR IRA
IN A SINGLE MEMBER LLC**

Another favorite strategy is to invest an unprotected IRA's a SEP-IRA or a deferred compensation plan's funds into a single member limited liability company (LLC). Your retirement funds then gain the LLC's "charging order protection." There are, of course, technical requirements, and your plan custodian must agree to this. Transfers of unprotected retirement funds to an LLC or partnership are also recoverable by a present creditor if it's a fraudulent transfer. So this strategy can fail if you have a present creditor and your IRA has no statutory protection. Still, a single member LLC is a reasonably good investment entity for unprotected retirement funds when the seas are calm.

**BOOST YOUR PROTECTION.
INVEST YOUR IRA IN AN OFFSHORE LLC**

For stronger IRA protection, move it offshore. Your IRA will be considerably better protected than in a domestic LLC. An alternate option is to transfer your retirement account to a sub-trust of a foreign asset protection trust (FAPT). But it's easier and less costly to have your fund custodian invest your IRA in a single member offshore LLC.

Here's how it works: Your retirement plan sets up a Nevis or Cook Islands LLC. Your IRA custodian then transfers your IRA funds to the foreign LLC in exchange for the foreign LLC's membership interest. Your IRA then owns the foreign LLC. Your IRA has *no* funds within the U.S., and your retirement account owns only the membership of the foreign LLC. This interest would be subject only to the creditor's charging order remedy.

You can be the LLC's investment advisor (and co-signatory on the foreign LLC account), until you have a judgment creditor when you would surrender control. Until then, you can safely reinvest the LLC funds in the U.S. If you are sued, a U.S. court cannot compel you or your custodian to turnover the retirement funds because the foreign LLC owns the funds, and this foreign LLC is controlled by a foreign manager and custodian.

If you have a large IRA that your state doesn't protect, use the foreign LLC. Unfortunately, few U.S. custodians are familiar with this offshore LLC strategy, but we have several qualified custodians well-experienced with this foreign LLC strategy. We have set up many offshore IRA – LLCs. All have successfully avoided creditor challenge.

BUY EXEMPT ANNUITIES
WITH YOUR IRA

Annuities are frequently exempt from lawsuits. So, if your state doesn't fully protect your IRA, you might invest your IRA in a protected annuity. We wouldn't ordinarily recommend buying an annuity for an IRA because it only duplicates your tax deferral advantage. However, buying a self-protected annuity for your IRA might be smart when asset protection is your primary goal. If so, buy a foreign annuity. You'll gain more protection if you buy your annuity from a foreign jurisdiction (Isle of Man, Switzerland, etc.) that fully protects their annuities. Purchase the annuity through the foreign LLC owned by your IRA as we discussed in the preceding strategy. For added protection, structure your ERISA pension plan payouts as annuity distributions.

TERMINATE YOUR IRA
AND PROTECT THE PROCEEDS

So you have an unprotected IRA and are sued? Your most practical solution may be to terminate your IRA, pay the tax (and early withdrawal penalties) and protect the proceeds as you would cash or other liquid assets. Terminating your plan is probably your most economical option if you have a relatively small IRA and can't cost-justify a more complex, expensive game plan. Also terminate your retirement account and protect the proceeds when the IRS is your primary creditor. The IRS seizes retirement accounts. Moreover, with your plan terminated, you can add the deferred IRA taxes and any early withdrawal penalties to whatever back taxes you already owe the IRS. You may settle all your tax obligations with the IRS as one "package." You might also borrow IRA funds from your IRA under IRS guidelines and temporarily protect the loan proceeds if the creditor threat will pass before you must repay your IRA. Don't touch your IRA, however, without first talking to your accountant or IRA specialist. There are too many rules, and you have to do things properly.

SAFEGUARD EVEN MORE
MONEY WITH A 412(I) PLAN

Here's one difficulty with most IRAs, even qualified plans: You can't shelter enough money. If that's your dilemma, then investigate a 412(i) plan. It can be your right answer if you're over 40, earn $250,000 or more annually, and have few employees. A 412(i) plan is creditor-sheltered under ERISA. And there are no limits on your annual contributions if the amount equals the premiums on the plan's insurance or annuities. You can also complete your plan funding over a short time period. The 412(i) is an excellent retirement tool if you're a higher income individual. It also offers excellent asset protection for high-income employers.

SHIELD YOUR IRA
IN BANKRUPTCY

So far, we've discussed retirement exemption planning in a non-bankruptcy context. However, when one files for bankruptcy the exemption rules change. Therefore, with exemption planning, one must consider the likelihood the individual will declare bankruptcy in the future. Even if bankruptcy is unlikely, one must plan for the contingency that it could happen. For example, an individual could be involuntarily petitioned into bankruptcy (Chapters 7 or 11) by three or more creditors if their aggregate claim exceeds $12,300, or even by one creditor if the debtor has fewer than 12 creditors, and the creditor filing the petition is owed $12,300.

Your state law determines whether you may use state exemptions only, or whether you may choose between the state or federal exemptions. If your state allows you to choose, then you may choose one set of exemptions, but not both. The federal exemption amount may be doubled for a married couple, although this may or may not be the case with state exemptions. Moving to a more exemption-friendly state before one files bankruptcy works only if you move at least 730 days (about 2 years) before filing.

Regardless of your state's exemption laws, retirement accounts are protected in bankruptcy, in aggregate up to $1 million. A court may increase this exempt amount "if the interests of justice so require." Unfortunately, this protection doesn't extend to SIMPLE or SEP IRAs. However, rollovers from other retirement accounts into an IRA generally enjoy unlimited bankruptcy protection and are not considered when calculating an IRA's value for purposes of determining whether you exceed the $1 million cap.

CHAPTER 6

FINANCIAL SELF-DEFENSE

FOR YOUR ESTATE & INHERITANCE

Why protect only what you own within your lifetime? Your financial self-defense plan must also protect those assets you'll leave behind when you pass on. Why work a lifetime to accumulate and safe-keep assets only to lose them after you die? Estate planning goes hand-in-hand with asset protection planning. That's why our firm specializes in both. We fully integrate our clients' estate and asset protection programs. Though estate planning is beyond this book's scope, let's highlight more common techniques that can shield your estate from claims and other avoidable losses.

PLAN
YOUR ESTATE

If you don't have a good asset protection plan, you probably don't have a good estate plan. Eighty percent of American adults have no will. We don't know whether you'll ever get sued. We do know you'll someday die. Without a good estate plan, your assets will likely pass to the *wrong* people or go to the right parties in the *wrong* way. Assets ending up with unintended beneficiaries are as wasted as assets seized by an undeserving creditor. And only a well-designed estate plan can save you estate taxes. A good estate plan will also help avoid conflicts that can only end in litigation. Create a conflict-free and lawsuit-free estate. Have as much of your wealth as possible go to your intended heirs. These good things happen only when you have a good estate plan.

You can't have only an estate plan. You can't have only an asset protection plan. You must integrate the two. Change one plan and you may need to change the other. The entities and strategies used for asset protection are also commonly used for estate planning. Many people who see us for asset protection have no estate plan, not even a simple will. Their need for asset protection prompted their estate planning. If you now have a good estate plan, we'll integrate it with your asset protection plan, or we'll work with your estate planning attorney to accomplish this. Integrating asset protection with estate planning also lets your arrangement take on a more "innocent" and defensible purpose; a particularly important tactic when your planning is done *after* you have creditors.

UPDATE YOUR ESTATE PLAN

An old estate plan can be worse than no estate plan. Keep your estate plan current and updated. You'll also need a comprehensive estate plan:

- Minimally, you need an up-to-date will (and/or living trust) so your estate doesn't pass by intestacy to unintended heirs.

- Beyond your will or living trust, you'll need a durable power of attorney (one for healthcare and one for your financial/legal affairs). You need someone who can immediately act for you if you become incapacitated. You also need a living will to spell out the circumstances when you want to artificially prolong your life. You can see why that's important.

- Find a good estate planner, particularly if you have a taxable or complex estate. A good estate planner can save you a fortune in estates taxes (when you die, Uncle Sam will likely be your #1 creditor). A good estate planner will also help you achieve your other estate planning objectives, including many you might have overlooked.

If the claims against you when you die are likely to exceed the value of your estate, then an asset protection attorney should work with your estate planning attorney so they may transfer to your heirs as much of your estate as legally possible – creditor-free.

CREDITOR-PROOF
YOUR ESTATE

Your next goal is to creditor-proof your estate. Most people fully pay their debts from their estates, but some estates have more debts than assets. You can also get sued *after* you die. So arrange your affairs so your assets pass to your heirs free of lawsuits and other adverse claims. Your heirs will appreciate your foresight:

- Title your property jointly or as tenancy-by-the-entirety, (if you want rights of survivorship). In most states, jointly-owned property passes to the surviving joint owner free of creditor claims against the deceased owner – if the creditor hasn't previously attached the property.

- Bequeath your property through an irrevocable trust funded within your lifetime. Do this before you have creditors.

- Make lifetime gifts to deplete your estate (provided the gifts aren't fraudulent transfers).

- Invest in fixed annuities or other financial products that transform your wealth into an income stream. The remainder interest would pass debt-free to your survivors.

- Use pay-on-demand (POD) designations to bequeath specific assets (IRA's, annuities, bank accounts), directly to beneficiaries.

A number of techniques – as well as financial products – can make your estate immune from creditors.

DON'T USE A LIVING TRUST TO LAWSUIT-PROOF YOURSELF

The living trust is America's most popular trust. The living trust lets you avoid the cost and delay of probate. But as the grantor, your revocable living trust will give you and your estate absolutely *no protection!* Your living trust can't protect your assets because it is revocable. You can change your living trust, as you can change your will. Since you can revoke your living trust, so too can your creditors. Assets in a revocable trust are always vulnerable to lawsuits!

Living trusts can sometimes cause you to *lose* lawsuit protection. For instance, some states don't homestead protect homes titled to a living trust (though most do). Check this. Similarly, assets owned by spouses as tenants-by-the-entirety lose their creditor protection from this type of co-ownership when those same assets are titled to their living trusts.

Expect trade-offs with the different options to title your assets. Select your *best* option. For example, why title your assets to a living trust? It's wiser to title your assets to a limited partnership (to lawsuit proof the assets) and have the limited partnership owned by your living trust (which avoids probate). When you die, the ownership of the limited partnership transfers through the living trust to your heirs without probate. Within your lifetime, your assets remain creditor-protected by your limited partnership. We have many other ways to use a living trust together with other entities to gain creditor protection and benefits from the living trust.

The grantor is ordinarily the living trust's income beneficiary. Upon the grantor's death, the trust assets go to the designated beneficiaries. Within his or her lifetime, the grantor controls the assets and can revoke or modify the trust. You may use one or several trusts for different beneficiaries or property. Your living trust may also be the beneficiary of pensions, insurance policies, Keoghs and other cash-value assets. Also a living trust won't reduce your estate taxes, though spouses sometimes use living trusts to maximize their estate tax credits. Other than the small cost to prepare and administer, a living trust has no disadvantages. A revocable living trust is definitely worthwhile if you have enough assets to require probate proceedings, and if you use it in combination with entities that *will* protect your assets.

DON'T LET YOUR CHILDREN LOSE THEIR INHERITANCE

Why do parents spend their lifetime scrimping, saving, and sheltering their wealth, only to leave their fortune to their kids who spend or lose it with their own lawsuits, bankruptcy, divorces, and so on?

If you gift significant wealth outright to your children, or other beneficiaries, it's foolish to leave their inheritance unprotected from their legal and financial problems. You might not want, or need, a trust to protect your assets from *your* creditors, but consider a trust to protect whatever assets you bequeath to your beneficiaries. This is particularly important when your children or grandchildren are your beneficiaries.

Irrevocable trusts can be *intervivos* or *testamentary*. You transfer your assets to an intervivos trust within your lifetime. You transfer assets to a testamentary trust upon your death. With a testamentary trust, your assets stay vulnerable to *your* own creditors until you die because only then do your assets pass to the trust. A revocable trust can protect the trust assets from your beneficiaries' creditors; but not your own. Whether you transfer your assets to the trust within your lifetime (an intervivos trust) or upon your death (a testamentary trust), the one major difference between a revocable and an irrevocable trust funded *within* your lifetime is that the revocable trust gives you – the grantor – no protection. Of course, other differences exist between the two types of trusts.

Your objective is to have a creditor-proof trust safeguard your beneficiaries' interest in the trust assets. For this, you'd incorporate trust provisions that prevent the beneficiaries' creditors from claiming their share of either the trust principal or income. "Anti-alienation" or "spendthrift provisions" directly protect the trust assets from the beneficiaries' creditors. The anti-alienation provision prohibits the trustee from transferring trust assets to anyone other than the beneficiaries. Excluded parties are creditors of the trust's beneficiaries. Spendthrift and anti-alienation clauses expressly preclude parties whose interest is adverse to the beneficiaries (a creditor, ex-spouse, IRS, etc.) from claiming the beneficiaries' share of the trust principal or income. Spendthrift provisions are vital for *every* trust. If the trust for your children lacks this protection, see your attorney, or *your* money could end-up with your ex-son or daughter-in-law, or your children's creditors.

MAKE TRUST
DISTRIBUTIONS DISCRETIONARY

Another important, but frequently overlooked protective trust provision is to give your trustee discretion to withhold income or principal distributions from the trust. For example, if your trust provides for your beneficiaries to receive trust distributions at age 25, how safe will those distributions be if your beneficiary has a judgment creditor or is divorcing at age 25? A discretionary clause lets your trustee withhold income and principal distributions that would otherwise go to the beneficiaries if the trustee thinks the distribution would be wasted or claimed by the beneficiaries' creditors. The discretionary clause also prevents a wasteful beneficiary from depleting or wasting trust assets. This too is an important point when your children or grandchildren are the beneficiaries.

If you worry that the money you entrust for your children may be squandered or claimed by adverse parties, add a discretionary provision to your trust so your trustee can regulate distributions to your children and avoid or minimize waste and creditor seizure. A beneficiary's creditor cannot force a trustee to distribute trust assets to the beneficiaries. A beneficiary's creditor can only claim payments actually received by the beneficiaries. However, the trustee can directly pay third parties on behalf of a beneficiary to circumvent a creditor seizing trust funds in the hands of the beneficiary.

Take it another step. Consider a "sprinkling" provision to your trust – particularly if your trust will remain in force for ten or more years and you can't accurately predict each beneficiary's future income or tax situation. The sprinkling provision lets the trustee modify trust distributions and disburse or retain principal and/or income for the duration of the trust. The trustee determines how much each beneficiary receives and when, following the grantor's distribution criteria set for the trustee. Minimum income distributions are required when the beneficiary is a spouse or dependent child. You cannot modify or revoke your sprinkling trust. Moreover, your beneficiary cannot be a trustee, or the trust assets would become vulnerable to the beneficiaries' creditors.

CHECK OUT DOMESTIC ASSET PROTECTION TRUSTS (DAPT), BUT YOU MAY NEED A STRONGER SHIELD

Alaska, Delaware and several other states have domestic asset protection trusts (DAPTs), which promise greater estate planning and asset protection benefits. The estate tax advantages are worth exploring, especially if your state has an inheritance tax. DAPT states primarily promote their trusts as an alternative to the offshore trust. Undoubtedly, many Americans are more comfortable using a domestic asset protection trust than a foreign trust, and this is their chief selling point. DAPT's are well-publicized. The Nevada DAPT is the most protective of the competing DAPT jurisdictions. Nevada trusts have the shortest statute of limitations for creditors to file claims. Still, Delaware trusts are most common.

Any well-drafted *irrevocable* trust can be an effective barrier against creditors of the trust grantor if the grantor is not also the beneficiary. In other words, the trust cannot be "self-settled." The trust must benefit a third party beneficiary. However, DAPT states allow self-settled trusts to protect against a grantor's (settlor's) creditors. Still, there are limitations and restrictions. A Delaware DAPT, for instance, must: 1) be irrevocable, 2) contain spendthrift provisions, 3) have at least one Delaware resident as trustee, 4) be at least partly administered within Delaware, and 5) the settlor cannot be the trustee.

The key question to answer before you set up any domestic asset protection trust is whether the DAPT will give you significantly more protection than a comparable trust in your own state. Moreover, will these trusts protect you against a *present* creditor?

DAPTs are *less* protective than offshore trusts because every state *must* recognize and enforce judgments and court orders issued from other states. Therefore, assets fraudulently transferred into a DAPT *may* be recoverable by a creditor from a non-DAPT state. This, and other issues about DAPTs, are far from resolved. Lawyers agree that DAPT protection against existing liabilities may be illusive.

There's another commonly overlooked problem. For a DAPT to be effective, the settler must usually reside within the state where the trust is formed. The trust assets must also be located within the state. If the trust's property is in another state, the law where the property is located will most likely prevail. For all these reasons, DAPTs may be less protective than suggested by their promoters. If you do use a DAPT, observe their statutory requirements, and add to the trust a provision authorizing the trustee to transfer or expatriate the trust to a foreign asset protection jurisdiction – if it later becomes necessary.

ACCELERATE YOUR GIFTS TO DEPLETE YOUR ESTATE

Lifetime gifting is a good way to reduce your estate taxes and protect the gifted assets if your gift goes to a liability-free recipient. You also save income taxes if the recipient is in a lower tax bracket. The annual gift exclusion lets you transfer $12,000 annually per recipient, tax-free, if your gift is immediately available to your recipient. If spouses jointly gift property, the exclusion doubles to $24,000 per recipient per year. A couple with three children can gift $72,000 annually tax-free. But for asset protection, you might accelerate your gifts. Here are some possibilities:

- Transfer your assets in exchange for a self-cancelling installment note (a SCIN) payable annually. You can forgive $12,000 each year, per recipient, without tax consequences. The note is thus self-liquidating. Since your gift would be a "fair consideration" exchange (the note), it wouldn't be a fraudulent conveyance. Title your note to a limited partnership to protect it from your creditors until it's fully liquidated.

- Bypass-generation gifts can accelerate your gifting, although these gifts can impose a generation-skipping transfer tax of 50% (plus the applicable gift tax). To avoid this, use a generation-skipping trust.

- Gift assets that are the most exposed to creditors. Retain assets that are either exempt from creditors or are otherwise well-protected, but also consider the assets you can gift most tax-advantageously.

- Transfer property to a minor child through a children or minor trust, or gift your assets under the Uniform Transfers to Minors Act. A minor's trust keeps the assets safe from the grantor's creditors, if the trust is irrevocable and the transfer to the trust not fraudulent.

CAUTIOUSLY USE
THE CHILDREN'S TRUST

To gift to minor children, consider an irrevocable children's trust. It can reduce your taxes. Assets not fraudulently transferred to a children's trust cannot be claimed by your future creditors. Nor will transferred assets be part of your taxable estate. Moreover, the trust income would be taxed at the children's lower tax rates, but keep in mind that the trust must stay in effect until the beneficiary is 21. Until then, the grantor, the child, and the child's creditors cannot claim the trust assets.

One disadvantage with the children's trust is that when your child reaches 21, your child can demand the trust assets. Since the trust is irrevocable, you cannot withhold distributions from the trust, nor prevent your child from claiming the trust assets. You can extend the trust until a later age only if your child, at 21, consents in writing, but can your child(ren) at 21 properly handle the trust assets? You no more want to lose the trust assets to an irresponsible 21-year old or to your children's creditors or ex-spouses, than to your own creditors.

CONTROL YOUR CHILDREN'S AND SPOUSE'S BEQUESTS WITH A Q-TIP TRUST

Control your estate from the grave and protect what you leave to your spouse with the Q-TIP (Qualified Terminable Interest Property) trust. When you die, your spouse gets a lifetime income from the trust. The trust principal passes to your children (or some other beneficiary) when your spouse dies or remarries. Q-TIP's are common in second or third marriages because they preserve the estate for the ultimate benefit of the grantor's children, rather than the spouse's children or family, who normally would become the beneficiaries if the deceased spouse's estate passed outright to the surviving spouse. However, Q-TIP's can be used for first spouses when the grantor is concerned that the spouse may waste the inherited assets during his or her lifetime. The Q-TIP essentially serves as a spendthrift trust to shelter assets from the spouse's creditors or subsequent mates. Q-TIP trust income must solely benefit the surviving spouse during the spouse's lifetime.

Estate taxes on the Q-TIP's funds are deferred until the surviving spouse's death. The Q-TIP won't protect the grantor's assets against his or her creditors because the Q-TIP is a testamentary trust. It's funded and effective only upon the grantor's death. The Q-TIP trust can shelter the wealth of a spendthrift spouse who might have future financial or legal difficulties.

GIFTING TO CHARITY? USE A CHARITABLE REMAINDER TRUST

Gifting assets is an extreme way to protect them. But you can give to charity, get protection, attractive tax benefits and draw income from these donated assets over your lifetime, if you gift through a *Charitable Remainder Trust* (CRT).

As the trust grantor, you select a tax-exempt charitable organization to be the beneficiary of the irrevocable trust principal. When you create and fund this trust, you make a charitable donation and can claim a tax deduction for the fair market value of the donated assets. You gifted the "principal," but you become the income beneficiary. Over your lifetime, the trust pays you an annual income. The net effect: you get an immediate tax deduction and enjoy lifelong income generated from your donated assets. With the tax savings, you can buy a life insurance policy, which gives your heirs the value of the donated assets or perhaps an even larger inheritance. There are a variety of charitable trusts. But don't simply gift your money to charity. Do it most advantageously for yourself, as well as for your charity. Talk to your estate planner or philanthropic gifting planner about the various planned gifting options.

DOUBLE THE VALUE OF YOUR LIFE INSURANCE WITH AN ILIT

Life insurance is an asset that often has a substantial cash value. Even a term policy can give your family vital income when you die. Life insurance can also pay your estate taxes, and make funds immediately available to your family without the delay or expense of liquidating assets. If you now own or plan to buy a life insurance policy, then protect it. Title the policy to an irrevocable life insurance trust (ILIT). An ILIT is an irrevocable trust specifically to hold life insurance. As with any trust, the ILIT has a trustee, beneficiaries and terms for trust distribution. Your ILIT owns the insurance policy on your life, and the trust is the beneficiary of each policy. When you die, the insurer company pays the ILIT trustee who distributes the proceeds to the ILIT trust beneficiaries. Your estate wouldn't be the beneficiary or it will pay estate taxes on the proceeds, and the money can be claimed by your creditors if your state laws do not fully protect insurance policies.

ILITs can either be funded or unfunded. An unfunded ILIT's, life insurance premiums aren't fully paid. You pay premiums to the trust which pays the premiums. A funded ILIT has either a fully paid insurance policy or sufficient income-producing assets to pay future premiums. Whether it's unfunded or funded, ILIT premiums should be paid directly from the trust. If the trust grantor directly pays the premiums, the grantor loses the trust's tax benefits and creditor protection.

As an irrevocable trust, the ILIT shelters both the policy's cash value and distributions from both the grantor's and beneficiaries' creditors. If life insurance is important for your family's financial security, and if life insurance isn't fully protected by your state's exemption laws, you'll need an ILIT for protection.

An ILIT is probably unnecessary for asset protection, but you may need one to save estate taxes. Since the ILIT owns the life insurance policy, the policy proceeds are *not* included in your taxable estate. For example, if you are single and die with an estate worth $3 million (including $1 million of life insurance proceeds), and there's a $2 million death tax exemption, your estate pays an estate tax on the remaining $1 million. The ILIT removes the $1 million life insurance from your taxable estate. You avoid all estate taxes. Moreover, the ILIT gives you more control over the policy proceeds than does an insurance policy owned outright. If you personally own your insurance, your insurer directly pays your policy beneficiaries. An ILIT, under your directives, controls *who* gets the proceeds and *how* and *when* the policy proceeds will be distributed.

BUY FINANCED LIFE INSURANCE TO EQUITY-STRIP YOUR ASSETS

Are you over 70 and health eligible? You can buy life insurance, finance 100% of the premiums, and use your assets as collateral. The insurance policy's cash value eventually covers the premium, and you have effectively debt-shielded your wealth. Your beneficiaries will inherit considerably more wealth when you die. Physicians, business owners and other high-income professionals find insurance premium-financing plans advantageous for both asset protection and estate planning. Can it make sense for you? Premium-financed insurance might be an excellent way to encumber your assets for several years and simultaneously immediately build your estate. However, as with any financial or legal strategy, it's not for everyone. You'll need the right life insurance professionals and estate and asset protection attorneys to help you decide whether, and how, it can best work for you. For more information on this, visit *www.AssetProtectionAttorneys. com.*

GIFT YOUR WEALTH TO YOUR CHILDREN, BUT RETAIN LIFETIME CONTROL

Parents with taxable estates oftentimes gift to their children as much of their assets as possible within their lifetime to reduce their taxable estate. Oftentimes, they also want to control the gifted assets. They certainly don't want to lose the gifted assets to their children's ex-spouses and claimants. One solution is to use a limited partnership and set up an irrevocable trust with spendthrift provisions on behalf of each child. You'd then gift a percentage of the limited partnership each year to each child's trust. As the general partner of the limited partnership, you continue to control the partnership assets. The gifted interest in the limited partnership would be sheltered by your children's spendthrift trusts. You can also accelerate your gifting because you get a discounted value on the limited partnership share that you gift to each child's trust annually.

DISCLAIM YOUR INHERITANCE IF YOU HAVE CREDITORS

If you expect a large inheritance, have judgment creditors or expect a divorce, disclaim your inheritance. A beneficiary can disclaim their inheritance and pass the inheritance on to the next generation. So, through a disclaimer, your children will get your inheritance and you won't lose it to your creditors. A disclaimer is a complete, unqualified refusal to accept property. You can disclaim gifts and inheritances. The alternate beneficiaries may be your children, a spouse, or anyone else you designate to receive the gift. Your disclaimer must be in writing, and you must not have accepted any part of the gift or any ownership benefits. Moreover, your disclaimer must be received by the transferor within nine months from the date of transfer or the creation of the document that gives you the future interest.

You have other ways to shield your inheritance. If you expect someone to leave you a significant inheritance, have them leave it to you through a spendthrift trust, or as a limited partnership interest, or domestic or foreign LLC membership. You then inherit a protective entity. An offshore trust is a particularly good way to pass on your wealth to the next generation and keep it safe from your own creditors and your beneficiaries.

SAFEKEEP YOUR WEALTH WHEN YOU'RE INCAPACITATED

Estate planning isn't only about death. Also ask who will manage your financial and legal affairs if you become incapacitated. Appoint someone who can responsibly manage these matters if you become disabled and can no longer act for yourself. You'll need a durable power of attorney (or "evergreen power of attorney"). Unlike ordinary powers of attorney, a durable power of attorney becomes effective, and stays in effect, *only* when you cannot act for yourself. The durable power of attorney insures that someone is continuously authorized to do whatever necessary to protect you and your assets. Your spouse or children don't have this authority. For example, your spouse cannot enter into important contracts on your behalf, commence or defend you against lawsuits, or transfer your assets, unless you authorize these actions through a power of attorney.

The only alternative to the durable power of attorney is to have a court appoint a conservator or guardian. But this can take weeks, or months, and it's expensive. You can always revoke a power of attorney, but appoint someone well-qualified to make the *right* legal and financial decisions for you. This individual may have different qualifications than one you would appoint to make your healthcare or other personal decisions.

INCLUDE A SENIOR TRUST IN YOUR ESTATE PLAN

We age and can gradually develop dementia and lose our judgment. We become vulnerable to those who may take advantage of our impairment. On the other hand, you don't want to lose control over your assets until you are certifiably incapable of handling them properly on your own. That's where the senior trust can help.

A senior trust requires a special trustee to join in decisions concerning the trust assets (including testamentary dispositions) once there is an irrevocability event. Until then, the trust remains revocable, and its assets completely within the grantor's control. A medical certification of dementia or mental impairment is usually that irrevocability event that transforms the trust from a revocable trust to an irrevocable trust and triggers the appointment of the special co-trustee. People lose assets due to the wrongful influence of family, friends, caregivers and business associates. The resultant loss is no less painful than losses to lawsuits or other claims. The potential tax issues must be handled carefully when you use a special trust, but the trust should be investigated by every senior as well as anyone else who questions their future ability to make the right decisions for themselves.

INTELLIGENTLY PASS ON THE FAMILY BUSINESS

The family business may be your primary asset. We have discussed techniques to protect your ownership interest in your business, but if you want to transfer your business to your children, retain control and maximum protection for your ownership interest. Here are some strategies:

- Contribute your interest in the business to a GRAT. This will provide you an annual payment for a set number of years. When the GRAT terminates, the remaining assets are distributed to the designated beneficiaries (your child or children, either outside or in trust). Your ownership interest can be transferred to the next generation with minimum gift tax liability. Depending on several factors, including the GRAT structure and the disposition of voting rights in the company stock, you could transfer minority interest(s) in the business while retaining voting control.

- Recapitalize your business into voting and non-voting equity. Subsequently gift the non-voting equity interests. If you apply the annual gift tax exclusion and lifetime gift tax exemption, you could (depending on values and timing) gift the non-voting interest tax-free. You'd retain all voting control.

- Sell your interest to an intentionally defective grantor trust (IDGT). Apply the discounts with valuing a minority interest in a family business and sell a minority interest in a business to a trust. You can immediately transfer your ownership interest to a trust for the eventual receipt by the beneficiary, avoid income and gift taxes, lock in a lower estate tax valuation, retain an annuity income stream, and divest yourself of an otherwise exposed asset-your ownership interest in the business.

CHAPTER 7

FINANCIAL
SELF-DEFENSE
FOR YOUR BUSINESS OR PROFESSIONAL PRACTICE

You personally need asset protection. So does your business or professional practice. It is even more vulnerable to litigation and creditor problems. It requires its own brand of financial self-defense. Unfortunately, few business owners go through the planning necessary to successfully blockade the inevitable financial threats that can sink their business. Businesses are the products of entrepreneurs and entrepreneurs are optimists. They go into business happily envisioning only the upside of their venture. They seldom see the downside. Ignoring the possibility of failure, they overlook the most basic precautions to protect their businesses should their rosy predictions fade. Realistic business owners don't wear rose-colored glasses. They know about and reduce their risks. They safeguard their enterprise. They shelter their personal wealth *and* their business, and they do it well before the inevitable lawsuits and creditor battles arise. These businesses are best positioned to survive in the turbulent times.

LIMIT YOUR PERSONAL EXPOSURE

How to organize your business? Should it be a sole proprietorship, corporation or limited liability company (LLC)? If your business has multiple owners, should it be a general partnership, corporation or LLC? (For now, consider the LLC the same as a corporation for liability insulation protection). Making the right decision is critical because what entity you choose determines your personal liability, as well as your business's exposure. There's also tax, financing, business succession, and a host of other issues to consider.

Which entity is best has no one right answer. You may also change organizational structure as your business grows. Today's entity may not be tomorrow's best. Your accountant and attorney should periodically review your entity because each type of organization has features, advantages and disadvantages. But high on your list of considerations is the need to limit your personal exposure from your business' inevitable debts and liabilities.

There's an easy case to be made *against* a sole proprietorship or general partnership. A sole proprietorship is operating your business without a formal legal entity – such as a corporation or LLC. As the sole proprietor, you are personally the business and are personally liable for *every* business debt. In these litigious times, why do so many small businesses still operate as sole proprietorships? Most small businesses fail, so why do their owners needlessly jeopardize their family's financial security? It's foolish. When these businesses fail, their owners face financial ruin because their business creditors will take their personal assets. Operating any business as a sole proprietorship or general partnership is *always* faulty planning!

General partnerships are particularly dangerous because the general partners are jointly and individually liable for partnership debts. Partners in a general partnership can easily lose their personal wealth if their business (or their partners) cannot fully satisfy the partnership obligations. Partnerships are a bad gamble. As you can see, the major disadvantage with the sole proprietorship or general partnership is that you have "inside-out" liability. Proprietorship or partnership creditors can go "outside" the business to satisfy their claims from the owners' personal assets. There's also "outside-in" exposure. The owners' personal creditors can seize business assets to satisfy the owners' personal debts. This isn't a sensible way to set up any business, even the smallest, seemingly safest enterprise.

You need a corporation or LLC to limit your liability. A corporation or LLC is a legal entity distinct from its owners. A corporation (or LLC) protects your personal assets from your business' debts and lawsuits. Because a corporation or LLC is considered a separate legal entity, its shareholders, directors or officers are not personally liable for its debts or lawsuits. If your corporation or LLC is sued or goes bankrupt, you'll lose *only* your investment in the business. Your personal assets will remain safe. That, in a nutshell, is why you need a corporation or LLC.

Some small business owners who start out as sole proprietorships or general partnerships become concerned only when their business is sued or goes bankrupt. The troubled business owner may then have one final opportunity to avoid personal liability by timely transferring their proprietorship or partnership assets to a corporation or LLC. This entity would pay down the "old" debts (for which their owners have personal liability). The newer debts would be corporate obligations (for which their owners have no personal liability).

No business is too small to need corporate or LLC protection, because no business is creditor or lawsuit-proof. Larger enterprises may have more need for corporate protection if only because they are bigger, but *no* business is immune from legal and financial troubles. Operate *every* business, enterprise, or activity through a protective entity. This is basic financial self-defense.

INCORPORATE IN NEVADA?

Where to incorporate? Corporate laws differ. There are advantages from incorporating in certain states. But where? If your corporation will actively operate in only one state, then incorporate in that state. Out-of-state (foreign corporations) must register in their home state. This subjects the corporation to their state laws. On the other hand, if you have flexibility, Nevada is a good choice. That's why so many businesses incorporate in Nevada.

Nevada corporations are state tax-free. Nevada doesn't share tax information with the IRS. Nevada corporate laws also offer more privacy (only officers and directors are public information). More importantly, Nevada corporate officers and directors are better protected. Nevada laws eliminate or limit the personal liability of officers and directors for breach of fiduciary duty (other than improper dividend payments). Nevada also imposes a short statute of limitations to sue for improper dividends. Important, too, is that Nevada allows director indemnification for directors who incur liability on behalf of their corporation. Insurance trust funds, self-insurance and granting directors a security interest or lien against corporate assets to guarantee their indemnification are all advantageous for liability protection. The authority of corporate officers and directors to lien corporate assets to indemnify themselves and obtain a priority claim against the corporate assets without the need to exchange funds can be a smart asset protection strategy. Other states invalidate such self-serving legal arrangements.

Another important new feature of Nevada corporate law is that their corporations can give you the same protection as an LLC. The corporate shares of corporations chartered elsewhere can be claimed by a stockholder's judgment creditors. Losing your corporate shares to a claimant can be disastrous if the stock has significant value.

Nevada now protects corporate shares against personal creditor foreclosure. This feature is particularly important with S corporations because foreclosed S corporation shares subject the corporation to loss of its S corporation status. This can possibly create a large tax penalty. The charging order protection for Nevada corporate shares treats Nevada corporations as a limited liability companies (LLC). It limits a stockholder's creditors only to the charging order remedy.

One downside to the Nevada corporation: They have twice the IRS audit rate of companies incorporated elsewhere. Wyoming corporate laws match Nevada's. That also is a good state for incorporating.

Delaware is another debtor-oriented corporate law state. They give many mid-size and larger corporations advantages, particularly in insulating directors and officers from stockholder claims.

ORGANIZE YOUR PROFESSIONAL
PRACTICE DEFENSIVELY

Businesspeople must protectively organize. So too must professionals. Professionals have several organizational options. Physicians, dentists, accountants, lawyers, architects, and other professionals may form professional corporations. However limited liability partnerships (LLP) and professional LLCs (PLLC) are becoming more popular alternatives.

A professional corporation, or some other limited liability entity, is necessary for today's professional. Though the professional may still be personally sued for his or her own malpractice, the professional corporation insulates the professional from personal liability arising from an employee's or associate's malpractice – as well as contract claims, employee lawsuits, and other practice-related liabilities against the entity. The corporation, as the employer (not the professional) would then be sued. Still, a surprising number of legal, accounting and physicians firms operate as general partnerships. If they incorporated, these firms would insulate each professional from the potential unlimited personal liability they can now incur because of their faulty organizational structure.

Professionals have several organizational possibilities. For example, each professional may form his or her own professional corporation. Their respective corporations could then create a partnership. Each corporation would be a partner. If the partnership incurs liability, the creditor's recourse is to go after the partnership assets. This would be the respective partner's corporations, and these corporations would have few or no assets. Each professional's personal assets would remain safe.

The professional corporation isn't always the professional's best organizational choice. However, a business corporation gives the professional one advantage over the professional corporation: The professional need not personally own a business corporation, but the professional must own the professional corporation. A business corporation may be owned by the professional's spouse or another protective entity (such as an LLC, trust or limited partnership).

A newer organizational option is the limited liability partnership (LLP). It is particularly suitable (and often limited) to attorneys, accountants and architects. Whether a professional can use a professional or business corporation, LLP or LLC depends on the profession. For example, chiropractors, in most states, can use a business corporation. Physicians and dentists, by state regulation, are usually limited to professional corporations or limited liability partnerships.

Which organizational arrangement is best for you? The answer depends not only on liability and risk avoidance, but also professional regulation, taxation, third-party reimbursement and accounting and operational considerations. What is certain is that today's doctor, accountant, lawyer and other professional can no longer simply set up shop without thinking seriously about how to protectively organize their practice.

AVOID DANGEROUS PERSONAL GUARANTEES

Are you a business owner who personally guarantees your corporate obligations? You reduce the corporation's usefulness as a liability-insulator. Banks demand the small business owner's personal guarantee, but you can sidestep personal guarantees to other creditors (and escape liability on existing guarantees) if you use common sense and adopt a tougher attitude. If one supplier demands your personal guarantee, find another. Most suppliers will give your corporation or LLC *some* credit without your personal guarantee. However, respect your creditor's concerns-reduce *their* risk. A supplier who refuses your corporation a $20,000 credit line without your personal guarantee may risk $10,000. Or the supplier may accept collateral – for instance, a security interest on your business or a guarantee from an affiliated corporation.

If you must personally guarantee a corporate debt, then negotiate for a partial guarantee. This limits your exposure. Insist that your creditor cancel your guarantee once your business establishes a track record for prompt payment. It's also foolish to guarantee existing debts. You gain nothing. If your business falters, creditors will want your personal guarantees. But why jeopardize your personal assets to secure a shaky corporate obligation? Don't assume your business will pay its obligations. Troubled companies seldom do. Also, have your partners sign whatever guarantees you sign. If you have fewer wealthy partners, expect the creditors to chase you for payment. So choose partners whose pockets are at least as deep as your own.

DON'T FORFEIT YOUR CORPORATE PROTECTION

Operating your business as a corporation or LLC won't guarantee that a corporate creditor won't sue you personally to collect a corporate debt. Corporate creditors oftentimes sue its corporate officers and stockholders.

Corporate creditors who try to pierce the corporate veil usually argue that their owners are *alter-egos* of their corporations. If you are that corporate owner, they'll succeed unless you follow basic corporate formalities. Correctly operate your corporation, or any other legal entity. Operate your entity independent of yourself individually, or any other entity. If a corporate creditor can successfully argue that you and your corporation function as one, you could lose your corporate protection.

Document asset transfers between you and your corporation, as well as transactions between related companies. If you operate as a corporation or LLC, your legal documents should say so. Put your corporate name and title alongside your signature on all documents. If you own multiple entities, have the officers and directors of the related corporations hold different positions, conduct separate corporate meetings, and maintain separate corporate books. Recording major director and shareholder actions is also important. Nor should you voluntarily dissolve your corporation if it has outstanding debts. These corporate debts then become your personal obligations.

Observe *every* corporate formality. Does your corporation have its own business address? Telephone number? Does your corporation pay its own expenses? Does it have the necessary business licenses? Checking and bank accounts? Each point establishes your corporation as a separate entity.

INSULATE YOURSELF AS A CORPORATE MANAGER

If you manage a corporation, LLC or any other entity, you can be personally liable for officer and director negligence, mismanagement, anti-trust and other regulatory infractions, as well as unpaid withholding taxes. Officers and directors incur personal exposure in many ways. How can you maintain management control while avoiding managerial liability? A few steps can minimize your exposure.

For the family business, only one spouse should be an officer and director, and this spouse should individually own few or no assets. Why expose both spouses to corporate claims? Make one spouse a safe harbor for the marital assets. Set up a management company to manage. An LLC doesn't need a natural person to be its manager, so a management company adds another layer of separation. An offshore management company imposes still more procedural obstacles. Offshore management companies provide on-site managers. Whether this is functionally practical depends on the size and nature of your business and the responsibilities you want the management company to oversee. Domestic firms also serve as nominee officers and directors for corporations (particularly Nevada and offshore corporations).

GET OFFICER/DIRECTOR LIABILITY INSURANCE

Corporate directors face many potential liabilities and must be protected by insurance. Directors need corporate indemnification and this must be secured by adequate director liability insurance. Publicly-owned corporations provide indemnification and insurance for their boards. Smaller, privately-owned corporations with outside directors may not. Few outside directors will serve on corporate boards without insurance, and directors won't pay for this insurance from their own pockets. Defending against claims becomes less complicated, tax write-offs for premiums less questionable, and policies less expensive when the corporation buys the liability insurance for its corporate board. A director is adequately protected only with the right insurance:

1. *Coverage:* Considering today's high litigation awards, you need at least $1 million coverage per occurrence ($5 million or more for larger corporations, or those with excessive risk, such as hazardous waste).

2. *Exclusions:* Does the policy cover such common claims as dishonesty, fraud, libel or slander, SEC violations, insider trading, pending lawsuits, ERISA, anti-trust and hazardous waste? Exclusions are negotiable.

3. *Deductibles:* A deductible of $5,000 per director, per claim is common. Other policies use split deductibles – 95% insured and 5% uninsured. A $5 million judgment is still a sizeable $250,000 loss to the director. You want affordable fixed-dollar deductibles.

4. *Notifications:* It's essential that the insurer notifies the directors if it cancels the policy.

5. *Supplemental insurance:* Can other insurance cover deductibles, exclusions and other lapses in policy coverage?

6. *Stability:* Is the insurer well-rated? Financially stable?

7. *Legal review:* Has your policy been reviewed and approved by both the company's attorney and your own? Your interests don't always match the company's.

AVOID PERSONAL LIABILITY FOR CORPORATE ACTIONS

Beyond D&O insurance, it's also important to know why you may get sued and avoid those pitfalls. Corporate directorships are increasingly hazardous, and directors can incur civil and criminal liability in many ways other than through negligent management. Here are nine chronic trouble spots:

1. *Improper dividends:* Dividends unlawfully declared make the directors personally liable to creditors for any resulting corporate insolvency.

2. *Shareholder loans:* Directors who vote for the corporation to make loans to an officer or stockholder are liable if they fail to repay.

3. *Unpaid taxes:* Corporate officers are usually responsible for unpaid U.S. withholding taxes. Certain states impose liability on directors for unpaid state taxes.

4. *Improper payments upon dissolution:* Directors are liable to creditors when they dissolve the corporation and distribute the proceeds to stockholders without fully paying creditors.

5. *Securities violations:* Directors are liable to investors for false and misleading statements in the corporation's prospectus. Outsider or unaffiliated directors must verify the accuracy of a registration. The SEC imposes this special burden upon them.

6. *ERISA:* The Employee Retirement Income Security Act imposes a director penalty of up to 100% of the funds involved in a prohibited transaction. Get a legal opinion before you undertake any ERISA transaction.

7. *Anti-trust violations:* Directors are personally liable for anti-trust violations that they reasonably should have been aware of. Liability can be particularly costly because you can be sued for triple the actual damages.

8. *Civil rights and discrimination violations:* This new source of liability for corporate directors arises when directors approve or allow corporate policies that violate these laws.

9. *Environmental violations:* Another growing problem
   for directors is hazardous waste – particularly when the
   directors actually knew about the hazardous waste problem.

An experienced corporate lawyer should represent the board
at every directors meeting. Sound legal advice can avoid
those wrong decisions that typically get directors into trouble.

SEPARATE YOUR
WINNERS FROM YOUR LOSERS

If it's smart to incorporate one business; then two, three or ten
corporations or LLCs are necessary to operate two, three or ten
businesses. Separately incorporate *each* business. One business
failure won't then endanger the others. This is how to creditor-
proof your growing conglomerate. The business graveyards are
full of once-thriving companies that operated as one corporation.
The smartest entrepreneur eventually becomes saddled with a
loser. That one loser can destroy a long string of winners. So,
isolate your potential losers from your present winners. You
want to more easily shed your losers and build on the strength of
your winners. Separate entities are essential when your business
is small and most vulnerable. Larger companies can't as easily
shed their losers because tax, financing, creditor, stockholder,
regulatory and operational factors require them to operate under
one corporate umbrella. Yet, you can lose the opportunity to
become big unless you can isolate your good ventures from the
bad. Many family-owned businesses operating under one banner
are, in fact, separate entities. If you own several businesses,
incorporate and operate each separately. Your numerous
corporations can be owned by your family's limited partnership,
or set up a holding company to own your operating subsidiaries

(corporations or LLCs). Your organizational possibilities are endless. However you structure your business, don't gamble *your* future on the improbability that *some* venture won't fail.

A corollary tactic: Divide one corporation into separate entities. Run your liability-prone activities through one corporation. Run your less dangerous activities through another. What's the heart of your business? Where and how is your business most likely to incur liability? How can you separate your potential problems from the guts of your business? This too is financial self-defense. This is the thinking that saves businesses!

TITLE BUSINESS ASSETS TO OTHER ENTITIES

Your next key strategy is to keep your operating company asset-poor. Expose as few assets as possible to claims if the business fails or if it is sued. For instance, if you own and use commercial real estate for your business, don't title it to your operating company. Why expose your valuable building to your business' creditors? Title the real estate to a separate limited liability company to keep it beyond the reach of your business' creditors. Common sense? Of course!

Your operating corporation probably owns other valuable assets. These too should be titled to outside entities. Equipment? Patents? Trademarks? Copyrights? Domain addresses? Distributorship? Franchise rights? Separately title these and any other valuable asset to a separate entity and lease or license these same assets back to your operating business. If your operating business fails, you can sell these assets, or use them to restart your venture. In either instance, they are preserved for *your* benefit.

That's how we organize businesses. Our clients' operating businesses own negligible real estate, equipment, trademarks, Web addresses, intellectual property, vehicles or other valuable assets. We title these assets to one or more separate LLCs (or foreign entities), and grant short term license/lease agreements back to their operating company. You'll need good corporate housekeeping so your business' creditors can't argue that these assets were commingled. These entities would then be considered one entity by the courts.

Document intercompany transaction. Investigate the possible tax benefits you might gain from these inter-company lease/licensing arrangements.

IS YOUR LOCATION IMPORTANT?
PROTECT THE LEASE

Your good location may be your most important asset. If so, protect your lease. You have options: Use a separate corporation to hold your lease. This corporation should have the right to sublet the space to your operating company under a monthly tenancy-at-will. If your failed business holds the lease (as is conventional), the bankruptcy court can sell the lease (even without landlord approval), and notwithstanding a lease that prevents assignments or lease transfers. In bankruptcy, you can lose your valuable location and your business, but if you hold the lease through one corporation and sublet to your operating company as a tenant-at-will, the company holding the lease can evict your failed business and sublet to a new start-up corporation. Or it can instead sell the lease and you profit from the sublet if you don't want to go back into business. In either instance, it's you, and not the creditors, who exploit the lease's value. When your lease is *not* an asset of your troubled business, its creditor's only option is to liquidate the business. When your creditors can't sell your business as a going concern at that location, you gain bargaining power to settle with your creditors for fewer dollars.

DEBT-SHIELD BUSINESS ASSETS

Again, those big, friendly mortgages! They're as important to creditor-proof your business as to protect your personal assets. Debt shields save businesses. A business heavily encumbered to a friendly lender gives you a tremendous defensive advantage. The $1 million business with a $1 million mortgage gives the mortgage holder priority over every other creditor. The business' general creditors can seize nothing. Your debt shield then gives your unsecured creditors no bargaining power, while you gain business-saving leverage. Elementary? Of course! This is the same strategy to shelter your personal assets.

For a debt shield to save your troubled business, your mortgage must roughly cover the value of your business. If you have too small a mortgage, your creditors have equity to seize. A friendly mortgage also gives you an important ally to combat your creditors, because the friendly lender can foreclose on your business and re-sell you the assets for a fresh start. A friendly mortgage effectively gives you more control over your business. Your mortgage holder can also finance your repurchase of the businesses assets with a new loan. But avoid sham mortgages. Your "friendly" mortgage must withstand scrutiny.

Who is your friendly creditor? It might be a relative who loaned you money to start your business, or a friendly supplier to whom you owe money. Be certain this supplier will cooperate in the tough times, or indirectly become the secured creditor to your own business. For instance, Nevada corporations are often "suppliers" to affiliated operating companies. The Nevada corporation indirectly has the same stockholders, but "nominee" officers and directors make the affiliation between the companies less detectable. The Nevada corporation can be owned by an offshore company for further privacy (but not for tax evasion).

However you accomplish it, you can't simply give a mortgage to a relative, friend or favored creditor. Be prepared to prove that you owe the money, and that it's an enforceable debt. As with any encumbrance against assets, the devil is in the details. Where do you find this lienholder? How do you create that enforceable debt? How do you pay the debt? How do you protect yourself from the lienholder? How do you get *enough* secured debt to cover the full value of your business? How might this friendly debt affect your other financing? How might other constituencies involved with your business react? What are the tax consequences? How can you use inter-company arrangements to create debt shields? When should you use a debt shield? Business debt-structuring is a sub-specialty of asset protection and we continuously develop new, more creative ways to debt-shield assets. We can structure one for *your* business through our *Wealthsaver®* program.

TURN BUSINESS ASSETS INTO CASH

Before closing shop, the troubled business' owners may want to strip whatever cash is legally possible from the business. They turn every asset into more easily protected cash. They distribute money to stockholders or shelter it through protective asset protection entities. You may, for example, sell or factor your accounts receivable. If your receivables are from creditworthy business customers, a factor will pay immediate cash for your receivables. Also you can cut your inventory. Troubled businesses can usually cut inventory to release fast cash, or you can sell or encumber your capital assets. Can you borrow more against your real estate or equipment? Can you sell and sale-leaseback these assets? Lenders oftentimes buy and re-lease equipment, vehicles and real estate. Finally, license or sell your proprietary assets. What valuable trade names, copyrights and patents can you sell? Can your company retain marketing rights? Proceed carefully. Creditors have rights. Avoid civil or criminal problems. Let a good lawyer guide you on these transactions, so you stay on the right side of the law.

RECAPITALIZE YOUR BUSINESS WITH LESS VALUABLE ASSETS

Your major challenge is not so much *how* to turn your business' assets into cash. It's how to *legally* extract that cash.

You can't be too casual here and run afoul of the law. Still, some techniques are workable for the family business. For example, you may *recapitalize* the business by contributing less creditor-attractive assets from an affiliated company in exchange for the troubled company's cash, or structure the transfer as an unsecured loan from the troubled company to the affiliate. The affiliate can also sell or license patents or other intellectual properties, or even capital assets (equipment, etc.) for the exchange. The troubled company's balance sheet doesn't change, only its assets and liabilities.

A fair value exchange (assuming that it arguably is) wouldn't be a fraudulent transfer, although creditors may certainly disagree. You can also reverse the transaction once the financial threat passes. Use corporations or LLCs – not individuals – for these exchanges. If individuals get cash from the troubled company (or other valuable assets), they may lose their own personal assets if the transaction is legally challenged. The efficacy behind this plan is its complexity. It's difficult for courts to value business assets. Multiple transactions, involving different companies, over a lengthy time period will more likely appear as transactions within the ordinary course of business. They are extremely problematic for creditors to successfully challenge.

"POISON PILL" YOUR CORPORATE SHARES

It's also important to make your corporate shares in the business worthless to your creditors.

One strategy is to impose transfer restrictions on your shares. Restrictions on share transfers generally won't stop creditors from seizing the shares, but reasonable restrictions might discourage the less aggressive claimant. Also assess your shares. If your shares are assessable by the corporation, a creditor who seizes your shares must pay these assessments. This reduces the value of the shares to the creditor by the amount of the potential assessment. Assessments are an excellent anti-creditor strategy. You can also issue irrevocable proxies. This assigns your right to vote your shares. Give the proxy to a relative, etc. If a creditor seizes your shares, the creditor can't vote your shares because you irrevocably assigned those rights to your proxyholder. This too significantly lessens the stock's value to the creditor who would have no voting rights. Exchange your voting shares for non-voting shares, or dilute your stock ownership. Why give your creditor a controlling interest in your business? For example, your corporation can sell more shares to other family members or to family-controlled entities (trusts, limited partnerships, etc.). It's a good idea to spread the ownership of the family-owned corporation between family members. No one family member should control the majority voting shares.

DON'T RUSH INTO CHAPTER 11

Don't hastily file Chapter 11 bankruptcy because your company has serious litigation, or lender or creditor problems. Most small companies don't survive Chapter 11. More companies would survive a non-bankruptcy workout. Why do so many bankruptcy attorneys file Chapter 7 (liquidating bankruptcy) or Chapter 11 (reorganization) when more effective, cost-efficient and faster methods can resolve creditor problems? Who knows? Our firm handles many non-bankruptcy workouts (in addition to asset protection planning) so we know these non-bankruptcy strategies that you can read about in *Turnaround: How to Turn Your Troubled Business into a Debt-Free Money Machine*. Goldstein (Garrett Press).

A business in financial trouble shouldn't rush into Chapter 11 reorganization for three important reasons:

1. An out-of-court workout is less costly than Chapter 11 reorganization. You'll pay huge professional fees to navigate your small business through Chapter 11. An out-of-court creditor arrangement can cut your fees by 80%.

2. An out-of-court workout keeps your financial information private. This is particularly important if you'll lose vital clients because of your financial instability. Employees also want secure employers. Out-of-court workouts give you confidentiality because it involves only you and your creditors.

3. You'll avoid Chapter 11's rules and restraints: A non-bankruptcy workout gives you more flexibility to design your repayment plan and also how you operate your business during the workout.

Still, out-of-court workouts aren't always your best alternative. A dissenting creditor can reject your settlement and sue your business, or petition it into bankruptcy. Holdout creditors often upset workout plans.

One alternative is the pre-packaged Chapter 11. Creditors accept your proposed non-bankruptcy repayment plan and agree that if you are forced to file Chapter 11, they agree to the same reorganizational plan under Chapter 11. A majority of your creditors can then accept an out-of-court plan. In Chapter 11, they'll force your settlement upon the dissident creditors. Your company can successfully and quickly emerge from Chapter 11 and save you time, aggravation and the huge legal fees of a prolonged Chapter 11.

CHAPTER 8

FINANCIAL SELF-DEFENSE

FOR YOUR OTHER ASSETS

You've seen the many possible ways to legally fortify your major assets. Now consider your other assets. They too are important. You can't overlook your bank accounts, expensive furniture, antiques, artwork, jewelry, accounts, lawsuit claims or intellectual property. Your "miscellaneous" assets may be your *major* assets. What can you do to protect them?

SHELTER YOUR BANK ACCOUNTS

Make it difficult for claimants to attach or freeze your bank accounts. If you have significant cash, open separate accounts through different entities in other states. Keep substantial accounts (over $500,000) in offshore financial centers, titled to an offshore trust or foreign LLC. However, a larger account might be well-protected when titled to a limited partnership. Spouses may safely title their cash in tenants-by-the-entirety accounts in states that protect T/E accounts. Never keep more money than you can afford to lose in any one account. And keep the balance under $250,000, so that it's fully FDIC insured.

If your smaller cash accounts are in imminent danger, spend down the account. Sprinkle cash gifts. (Small transfers are usually unchallenged as fraudulent transfers). Reduce the debts against exempt assets such as your mortgage on your homestead protected home. (Check your state laws). Buy exempt assets with your spare cash. Pay friendly, preferred creditors. (Stay out of bankruptcy to avoid a preference). Pay debts non-dischargeable in bankruptcy (student loans, fines or taxes). Or prepay future expenses (car loans, college tuitions, insurance, etc.). You can also lend money to an entity (usually without assets) owned by another family member in exchange for a long-term unsecured note. Your creditor can claim the note, but it will have little value to the creditor when the repayment remains years away.

TITLE YOUR COLLECTIBLES
TO A LIMITED PARTNERSHIP

Household furnishings usually have negligible value to creditors. But you must shield precious artwork or antiques.

Most states partly protect household furniture from creditors' claims under their state exemptions. However, valuable antiques, heirlooms, art, expensive carpets, pianos, electronics (stereos), jewelry (including watches), and valuable collections (stamps, coins) need protection.

Six alternatives:

1. Sell or pawn exposed personal assets and dispose of or protect the cash proceeds.
2. Transfer these assets to a family limited partnership, particularly if the assets may increase in value, or be viewed as investments.
3. Title the items to the less vulnerable spouse.
4. Exchange these assets for exempt assets of equivalent value.
5. Transfer the assets to an irrevocable trust.
6. Encumber these assets, as you would other assets.

Co-owning these assets can make it more procedurally difficult for creditors to seize them. Partial interests may be virtually worthless. For example, if you have a painting worth $20,000 and sell a 50% interest to your friend, your 50% interest becomes worth far less than $10,000. It's difficult to re-sell a one-half interest.

Never conceal or hide your assets – no matter how inconsequential the item's value may be. It's a serious bankruptcy offense. Creditors discover expensive jewelry, valuable artwork and other precious assets through your insurance policy's special riders that specifically cover these valuables.

INCORPORATE YOUR SAFE DEPOSIT BOX

What's inside *your* safe deposit box? Inquiring minds want to know!

Your safe deposit box isn't safe if a claimant suspects it contains cash or other valuables. Judgment creditors can gain access to your safe deposit box. So can the IRS. They can also seal your box and deny you access until they examine its contents. The IRS and state taxing authority can also impound your box when you die. The answer is to rent your safe deposit box through a corporation. Give someone you trust co-signatory authority to the box. Judgment creditors will ask about safe deposit boxes (always answer honestly), so before creditor examination, give a third party the key and signature authority to the box. It's best to surrender any relationships you have to *any* safe deposit boxes to which you were previously connected. And don't hide cash or valuables in your safe deposit box. A safer strategy is to rent an offshore safe deposit box or even an oversize vault in "vault banks" in foreign privacy havens. These vaults are useful to hold gold, silver, precious metals and to safe-keep sensitive information, such as trade secrets.

TITLE YOUR VEHICLES TO AN LLC

Your automobiles, boats and other vehicles are probably a small part of your net worth, yet these assets will be one of the first creditors investigate. Title or lease your vehicles to the less-wealthy spouse if you're married, but it's smartest to title or lease vehicles to an LLC. This will better protect you against the uninsured accident.

For protection, you can fully refinance your vehicles, if and when it's necessary, so little or no equity is available for creditors. Refinancing is the easiest way to protect these assets.

Autos, boats, airplanes, recreational vehicles and other vehicles generally won't interest creditors if they have loans against them for 75% or more of their value. Vehicles seldom yield more at auction. Never co-own vehicles. This only expands your liability. Co-owners (usually spouses) have joint liability if their vehicle is involved in an accident. If your children drive your car, title it to an LLC or you'll be sued if *they* get into an accident. Buy a $2 million auto liability umbrella policy in addition to your standard liability policy. Finally, consider leasing your car. Your creditor then has nothing to chase.

BLOCKADE CREDITORS FROM MONEY DUE YOU

Your assets may be in the hands of a third party. Accounts receivable, tax refunds, cash value life insurance and annuities are examples. As with wage attachments, these assets can be seized through court-issued assignment orders, which direct those holding funds due you to pay your creditors instead. Creditors uncover third parties who hold assets due to you through various asset discovery procedures.

How can you blockade an attachment order? Your best alternative: Induce these third parties to pay you *before* the creditor wins its judgment. Accelerate payment. Offer them an attractive discount for prepayment, or, assign any monies due you to another entity, such as a limited partnership or limited liability company. A third alternative is to sell your receivables or future income anticipation to a factor or structured settlement company. They might pay you more than you would expect! Or sell any obligations due you to investors, but sell these assets for their fair value to avoid a fraudulent transfer claim. Your final option: Pledge these receivables as collateral for one or more loans.

Nor should you forget the claims you may have against others. This may include pending lawsuits where you are the plaintiff. These claims can similarly be sold or assigned to others who will pay you for your claim.

SIDESTEP WAGE GARNISHMENTS

Judgment creditors can seize paychecks with a *wage garnishment*.

What portion of your paycheck your creditor can claim is limited by federal and state laws. Each state protects wages differently. Debtor-friendly states fully exempt wages from creditor garnishment. New York shelters 90% of net wages. Only 10% (in aggregate) can be claimed by a debtor's creditors. As with the homestead laws, you must follow your state procedures to protect your wages. For instance, some states require wages to be segregated in "wage exemption" or "wage earner" accounts to avoid commingling your protected wages with unprotected funds.

The federal Consumer Credit Protection Act (CCPA) limits wage garnishment to the lesser of : 1) 25% of the debtor's disposable income per week (disposable income is the net paycheck after deducting federal and state withholding and FICA wages), or 2) the amount by which your weekly disposable income exceeds 30 times the federal minimum hourly wage. Exempt (protected) income cannot be garnished once you receive it, provided you keep it segregated from your other monies.

You can temporarily avoid garnishment. Form a corporation and direct your income to the corporation under an independent contractor arrangement. For tax purposes, draw the money out as a loan. This simple strategy is sometimes used by debtors to temporarily shield non-exempt wages, but it's seldom a practical long-term solution. Moreover, most employers will rightfully resist this arrangement if it violates IRS rules and, in reality, it is an employer-employee relationship. Another wage protection strategy is to make a prior wage assignment to a "friendlier" creditor, who can then periodically "loan" you money. Wage assignments must be in writing and in force before other creditors get their garnishment order. To defend the assignment's validity, prove the validity of the obligation. The IRS isn't subject to wage attachment laws and can leave you with less of your paycheck. Nor are wages protected from child/alimony support orders. If you have a significant, continuing wage attachment, it usually will force you to resolve the debt through bankruptcy, settlement or work stoppage.

CHAPTER 9

FINANCIAL
SELF-DEFENSE
AGAINST
LAWSUITS

Our passion to lawsuit-proof people is because we've seen the financial and personal devastation caused by lawsuits. Lawsuits have become epidemic and they will only become a bigger problem. The future will bring still more lawsuits and bigger awards. Litigation is America's fastest growing business. Few of us aren't victimized by one or more major lawsuits. There are fifty million new lawsuits filed annually. But this is only one dismal statistic. Many more lawsuit defendants are involved because one lawsuit can ensnare multiple defendants.

Why do so many people sue? Why not? It costs them nothing if they lose their case, but a few hours of their time. And they gain so much if they win. Why work when you can sue your way to wealth? Why play the lottery or Vegas slots when your odds of winning are much better by gambling in court?

More frightening than the sheer number of lawsuits are the ridiculous cases that wiggle their way through the courts. Litigation has turned into its own form of entertainment. Even when you can endure the odds of being sued, and the uncertainty of whether you'll win or lose, can you chance a devastating judgment? You can't predict what you'll lose in a lawsuit. A plaintiff can win a few dollars in actual damages and pocket millions more in punitive damages. A buyer of a defective $20 product can spark a billion dollar class action. One lawsuit turns into an avalanche. Enough nuisance lawsuits have toppled the most powerful businesses and wealthiest families.

That's why nine out of ten lawsuits settle. No defendant can go to trial confident of victory. No defendant can foresee what he'll lose. Few defendants can afford the exorbitant legal fees.

These realities encourage plaintiffs' lawyers to use lawsuits to extort whopping settlements. The economics are always with the plaintiff. The defendant is coerced to pay "go away" money because a defendant with exposed wealth has too much to lose. Financial self-defense levels the playing field. You're a less attractive lawsuit target. You negotiate faster, less expensive settlements. You protect your wealth against devastating losses. No less important – you reduce your anxiety once you secure your wealth.

Of course, you'll try to avoid lawsuits. Still, you can be reasonable, avoid situations that might get you into trouble, pay your debts and your taxes, avoid marriage and never start a business; still it would be ridiculous to think you'll be lawsuit-free. There'll always be lawsuits. Since you can't avoid lawsuits, you must protect yourself from them. When you're properly protected, you can live life with less worry about being sued and losing what you have worked so hard to build.

USE YOUR PROTECTION AS A
SELLING POINT TO SIDESTEP LAWSUITS

The ultimate asset protection goal is to give yourself and your family the confidence that you can't lose your wealth to any financial or legal problems. Good asset protection *discourages* lawsuits. To discourage lawsuits, convince a potential plaintiff that they can't seize your wealth even if they win their lawsuit. Discourage one lawsuit and you avoid the devastating cost to defend against that lawsuit. Prevent one lawsuit and you'll pay for your asset protection many times over.

Litigation is economics. A potential plaintiff must consider what it will cost to sue you. What are the odds they'll *win* and recover based on your *exposed* assets? In other words – *are you worth suing?* Few prospective plaintiffs sue once they see they can't recover more than their cost to sue! Lawyers want profitable cases. You might still get sued because every lawsuit has some "settlement value." You'll pay "something" to make the lawsuit disappear, if only to avoid legal costs. Call this extortion, but that's our legal system. Or someone may also sue you "vindictively." They have a score to settle. You may also be a side defendant in a lawsuit. Your wealth isn't checked by the plaintiff because you're only one of several defendants. If you're the primary lawsuit target, your ability to pay a sizeable judgment becomes a key factor in the lawsuit decision. Most often, it's not whether you have assets that determine whether you get sued; it's whether you have *exposed* assets. You must convince a prospective plaintiff that you have an *impregnable* financial fortress. Nine out of ten prospective litigants then won't sue!

NEGOTIATE
INEXPENSIVE SETTLEMENTS

If you're sued and if your assets are well-protected, you are in a strong position to negotiate a fast, inexpensive settlement. Negotiate from a position of strength. Let your opponent *know* you have nothing to lose, and they have little or nothing to gain from their lawsuit. Most plaintiffs won't know that you're shielded until after they sue and your attorneys talk. A good defense lawyer sells the reality that you're judgment-proof. Your goal is to settle the lawsuit quickly and inexpensively. Plaintiffs also realize they'll have attorney fees – 25% to 50% of any recovery. And the creditor isn't always sure about his legal position. A litigant will also wait years for trial. Why go through all this when you are judgment-proof?

The trick, of course, is to become judgment-proof so you can prove you have no exposed assets, or you may have multiple creditors. If so, more negotiating tips: Sincerity, quick action and close contact with your creditors are vital to build credibility and reduce hostility. Prepare accurate financial statements before you negotiate. Truthfully reveal that you have few or no exposed assets. If other creditors hold priority claims, sell this point, too. Treat your unsecured creditors equally. Give each a proportionate settlement. Give no one creditor a better deal. Be flexible. Will you pay a lump-sum settlement or installments? Will you pay interest? Give security? You have points to negotiate. Be realistic. Don't settle if you can't honor your deal. Bargain for a lower settlement if that's all you can pay. Persist. Creditors may not initially accept your offer, so try again. If you can't convince a creditor to settle, can your attorney? Can influential larger creditors persuade smaller holdouts? And negotiate for more than a release. Protect your credit. Have your creditors agree not to file a negative, late payment mark against you.

ARBITRATE OR MEDIATE FOR A FASTER, CHEAPER RESOLUTION

Litigation is expensive, cumbersome and time-consuming. That's why alternate dispute resolution (ADR) mediation or arbitration is fast replacing the courtroom battle. A mediator opens communication and encourages settlement. Arbitration makes final binding awards. Testimony is presented at a hearing overseen by an arbitrator who arbitrates under American Arbitration Association rules.

Nearly every civil case today goes through mandatory mediation because the courts want to settle as many cases as possible. Certain cases require arbitration by statute, but usually the parties agree to binding arbitration within their original contract. However, you can agree to arbitrate once a dispute arises.

Arbitration isn't always preferable for a defendant because arbitration moves rapidly. Litigation can be prolonged for years. Time is always a bargaining chip for the defendant. On the other hand, arbitration can lower your legal fees, avoid punitive damage awards, and put your case before a panel of arbitrators. They are likely to render a fairer verdict than a jury.

CREATE BULLETPROOF CONTRACTS

If you can't avoid lawsuits, you can minimize the dangers of being sued. Give yourself a decided advantage should there be litigation. C.Y.A. with every possible protective clause in your legal documents. Get a lawyer to draft every legal form, invoice, employment application and the hundreds of other forms, contracts and documents you'll need to deal with your customers, employees, vendors, etc. Write in terms that protect you! You can't afford sloppy paperwork. Review the documents and boilerplate contracts used by your bigger competitors. They know what fine print can also work for you. They have those protective provisions there for a good reason. Borrow them. Protect yourself!

WEIGH THE OVERALL ECONOMICS

If you lose a lawsuit, you'll owe more than what the judge or jury awards the plaintiff. You'll also owe interest on the award. Interest starts from the day the lawsuit is filed. Civil trials can end years after the lawsuit is filed. You'll then owe years of interest, plus the awarded amount. Interest rates vary by state, but range between 5% and 18% annually. If your state imposes a 12% interest (about average) and you're liable for $50,000, after five years of litigation you'll owe $38,000 in interest – or a total of $88,000! Add legal fees, witness expenses, court costs, transcripts and the time you spend not making money and you can see litigation's true cost.

Consider these economics when you negotiate settlement. Minor lawsuits can end up literally bankrupting the defendant.

REDUCE THOSE HEFTY LEGAL FEES

Win or lose a case, but expect huge legal bills. America is one of a few countries where a successful defendant pays his own legal fees and costs. England, and most other countries whose legal systems are similar to our own, has the loser pay the victor's legal fees. In America, each party pays its own fees and costs, unless a contract or special statute says otherwise. You can "win" your lawsuit and still owe thousands, or millions, in legal fees and costs. This is no victory! And legal fees are skyrocketing. Lawyer overbilling is alarmingly rampant. You can try to keep your assets safe from your adversary, yet lose a big slice of your wealth to your own lawyer. You must limit your legal costs *before* you do battle, or you'll lose the war even if you win in court.

Avoid big name lawyers. Every community has a lawyer or two reputed to be the best hired guns in town. But few attorneys with golden reputation are worth their excessively steep fees – particularly when a junior associate will handle much of your case. Hire an attorney experienced with your type case, a lawyer who'll respect your need for an economical, fast, and relatively painless resolution. Also shorten the battle. Lawyers can needlessly prolong any case. Endless depositions and court appearances are tactics that only generate horrendous legal bills. You get no corresponding benefit. Watch your lawyer's clock. You largely control your legal costs if you control your demands on your attorney. Still, lawyers pad their bills, churn needless work and mount billable hours. The non-lawyer can't easily determine what fees are reasonable. If you're in doubt, let an impartial lawyer review the legal services and the fee. The opinion should come from someone who can objectively assess the services and fees without a stake in what you'll do with that advice. Finally, talk honestly with your lawyer if you feel overcharged. If you still are unsatisfied, arbitrate the fee through the state bar fee arbitration committee.

MAKE A GOOD OFFENSE
AS YOUR BEST DEFENSE

More important than an inexpensive lawyer is the lawyer who can and will fight like a tiger. Your lawyer must counterpunch. Make it painful for the plaintiff to sue...or continue the fight. Can you counterclaim? Who else can you drag into the fray? Can you swamp your adversary with discovery? Can you depose others who your adversary wouldn't want involved? Can you raise embarrassing facts that your opponent wants buried? Is your lawyer clever enough to run up your adversary's legal fees while holding down your own? Don't be a punching bag. Throw a few right hooks yourself. Put on your own boxing gloves!

HOLD YOUR LIABILITY
INSURER RESPONSIBLE

If you are sued and you have liability insurance, keep your insurer on the hook. Your insurer must defend you in good faith or you can sue them for any judgment against you above your coverage. Your insurer can have liability for excessive awards unless it notifies you of the excess claim and settles or attempts to settle the claim in good faith within the policy limits. Your insurer can't refuse a reasonable settlement which exposes you to liability above your insurance. Insurance companies decline claims coverage, but if you question your coverage, demand that your insurance company defend and indemnify you. Your insurer may defend the claim and reserve the right not to pay any award. Or your insurer may litigate its liability under your policy. If you have potential exposure beyond your insurance coverage, hire your own attorney to protect you against an excessive award, as well as to assert your rights against the insurer. The attorney retained by the insurance company has the duty to defend you, but remember, your interests and your insurers may conflict.

STOP SEIZURE OF YOUR ASSETS

A judgment creditor seizes your assets by *executing on their judgment*. The specific processes vary by state, but typically, for real property, the creditor files a summary of judgment in the county recorder where your real property is located. This "liens" the property to the amount of the judgment. This lien is valid against any real property owned in your own name in that county at the time, as well as any future acquired real estate. You can't sell or refinance liened property(ies) without satisfying the judgment. Thus, a lien effectively ties up your real estate until you pay the judgment or settle.

Personal property is seized through levy. The sheriff or marshall physically takes the property described in the levy, whether directly from you or from a third party. This includes money in bank accounts, items in your safe deposit box, automobiles, jewelry, antiques, collectibles, equipment, or any other unprotected physical assets. The sheriff converts property to cash through a sheriff's public auction.

Wages are seized by a levy or garnishment. The creditor's levy orders your employer to send your pay to the creditor (except for the legally protected exemption).

If a creditor is about to take your assets or garnish your wages, you must immediately take three steps to protect yourself. First, file a claim of exemption to protect your exempt assets. Each state lists assets a creditor cannot take. This includes tools of the trade, household items and specified personal property. Federal law provides further exemptions. You'll need to file a claim of exemption to properly shield this exempt property. Their protection is not automatic. Second, pay the judgment or settle; perhaps you'll pay over time. Negotiating settlement saves the creditor foreclosure hassles and you get to keep your property. Your third option, file Chapter 7, 11 or 13 bankruptcy *before* the auction. Bankruptcy has serious consequences, but it will stop a forced sale of your assets. If you plan bankruptcy, do it *before* seizure and sale to save your assets.

DON'T FORGET OLD JUDGMENTS

A judgment creditor can collect for a certain number of years. Most states enforce judgments for 20 years. Wyoming and Kansas, for instance, allow creditors five years to collect on a judgment. Creditors can extend their judgment, usually for one term equal to the original. A 10-year judgment thus becomes enforceable for 20 years. Some states allow the creditor to continuously extend the collection period. These judgments never expire. Creditors can then pursue your estate, unless you go bankrupt or settle. Take a judgment seriously.

Never drop your guard. Don't accumulate assets on the erroneous belief that an old judgment creditor can't pursue you. Judgment creditors may temporarily disappear once they see you have no exposed assets, but may renew the chase once they discover your new-found fortunes. Whenever you have a judgment against you, discharge your debt in bankruptcy, settle, or follow a strict protection program over your lifetime.

PROTECT YOURSELF BEFORE
YOU EXPECT A LAWSUIT

In certain circumstances, your assets can be attached pre-judgment. A pre-judgment attachment secures collection of a future judgement by encumbering your assets so you cannot dispose of them to your creditors' detriment.

A court considering a pre-judgment attachment, will balance two issues: 1) Is the plaintiff likely to win the suit, and 2) Is the defendant likely to dispose of his assets before the judgment – if the attachment is denied?

The court balances the right of the defendant's full use and enjoyment of his property until final judgment against the right of the alleged creditor to assurances that enough assets will be available to satisfy a future judgment.

Courts more commonly award pre-judgment attachments on contract claims, such as suits on promissory notes or for claims of unpaid goods or services. Attachments are normally denied on more speculative claims, such as negligence cases. For a pre-judgment attachment, the creditor may be required to post bond to reimburse the defendant for losses caused by the attachment, should the defendant win.

Federal agencies routinely obtain pre-judgment attachments or "freeze orders" to freeze a defendant's assets even before the defendant is served the lawsuit. So you must protect your assets before you have problems. Never assume you are safe *before* judgment enters against you. You can lose the opportunity to protect your assets at any time and without warning or advance notice.

CHAPTER 10

FINANCIAL SELF-DEFENSE FROM FORECLOSURES

Our bad economic times are yielding an avalanche of real estate foreclosures, as well as repossessions of cars, boats and other personal property. What do you do when you can't pay your loans? What self-defense measures must you take when your bank forecloses on your home or business? How you handle your secured lenders requires far different strategies than you use with other adversaries because your secured lenders are in a more powerful position: They hold liens against your assets. Still, that doesn't mean you can't defend yourself, or intelligently resolve your situation to your advantage. You can. You must, however, approach the problem from a different direction and attempt to carve a win-win situation between yourself and your lender. Your resolution must give you and your lender the most favorable outcome possible. Here are some ideas.

TALK TO
YOUR LENDER

If you're inexperienced with problem loans, you may fear your problem. Playing ostrich is common and also costly. Lenders are less patient with borrowers who avoid their problems. They'll more likely cooperate with borrowers who confront their difficulties, negotiate fair, interim arrangements, and try to reach a reasonable long-term solution advantageous to both parties.

Scan the newspapers. Homes, investment properties, cars, boats and other assets routinely fall under the auctioneer's hammer. We know the reasons for financial trouble. A poor economy. Rising interest rates. Job losses. Business failure. Personal problems. You borrowed too much and now owe more than the value of your home or collateral. Or your loan is poorly structured, and you must adjust your loan to what you can afford. The defaulted loan might require major restructuring. You may need to reduce your debt and/or extend or modify your payments to your financial abilities. What you *can't* do is resolve your problem by ignoring it.

UNDERSTAND FROM
YOUR LENDER'S VIEWPOINT

Foreclosure or repossession might cause you to lose your home, business or other property. You may also have a deficiency on the loan and still owe your secured lender a balance. This jeopardizes still more assets. Your strategies are much the same whether your loan involves real estate, boats, cars or apartment complexes. The lender is secured by certain assets as collateral. The lender can sell the collateral and apply the sale proceeds to the loan. The surplus is yours. If there's a deficiency, you'll owe your lender the difference. A secured lender with enough collateral is in a stronger position than the unsecured creditors who must first sue you and win a judgment before they can seize assets. In bankruptcy, your unsecured creditor may get little or nothing. Your secured creditor has the pledged collateral.

So your secured lenders are in a more powerful bargaining position, but you can still negotiate an asset-saving deal with your lender when you can't pay your loan. Lenders don't want your collateral. They want payment. Lenders don't want foreclosure hassles. And foreclosure reflects poorly on the lender's judgment in making the loan. It also reflects poorly on the borrower. Still, no lender can remain idle while your loan falls further into default. Lenders and borrowers in loan workouts must understand each others position. They must compromise and cooperate until they resolve their mutual problem. Final resolution may be new terms, new financing, or the debtor voluntarily surrendering the collateral to the lender.

Some loan workouts are creative. However it works out, you must convince your lender that you're in good faith, and trying to protect the lender as much as saving your assets. As a borrower, you also must protect yourself from your secured lender. Lenders can be unreasonable. You must know when to cooperate and when to fight.

SHELTER YOUR OTHER ASSETS, THEN BATTLE YOUR LENDER

Never battle your lender while you have unprotected assets. Your lender will go after these assets to secure their shaky loan. Of course, you want to protect these assets from your lender *before* you borrow. This protects you against a later fraudulent transfer claim. Also protect any money you have on deposit with your lender.

When your loan defaults, your lender will demand more collateral. Refuse! If your lender questions whether the present collateral will cover the loan, it probably won't. Why jeopardize more of your assets? It only improves your lender's bargaining position and weakens yours. Nor will withholding more collateral trigger faster foreclosure. The well-secured lender can confidently foreclose. They know they have enough security to fully cover their loan. The poorly-collateralized lenders hesitate to foreclose. Only time gives them the chance to recover more. Gracefully refuse your lender's demand for additional collateral. You have reasons. Perhaps your other properties are titled to your spouse. You'd grant the lender's request, but you're having marital problems and your spouse won't agree. You get the idea! You have many face-saving ways to politely refuse your lender – and still appear cooperative. Poverty, strangely, is power. A lender with too few assets to fully recover their loan greatly improves *your* negotiating power.

FIND THOSE
FATAL LOAN DEFECTS

Don't assume that your lender has an enforceable mortgage. A host of possible legal defects in mortgages can make the mortgage worthless (but not necessarily the obligation). Defects or technical problems can significantly delay foreclosure. Is your mortgage defective? Have your loan transaction reviewed by an attorney. Some defects will make the mortgage or security interest void against third parties, but not the debtor. Bankruptcy, Chapter 11, an assignment for the benefit of creditors or similar insolvency proceeding are transfers to a third party that may void a defective mortgage or security interest. A defective mortgage holder can also lose their collateral to subsequent lien holders. Uncover those serious mortgage defects and you have bargaining leverage with your lender – particularly if your cooperation is necessary to correct the problem.

WAIVE THE
LENDER LIABILITY CLUB

Perhaps your lender didn't play by the rules. A lender liability lawsuit can be a formidable weapon in the beleaguered borrower's arsenal. Courts sanction lenders for lending violations. Lenders despise lender liability claims because a borrower might win huge damages and cancellation of their loans. The most common violations: Fraudulent lender conduct or misrepresentations when soliciting or administering a loan, changing loan terms without borrower consent, unreasonable control over a borrower's collateral, failure to make agreed loan advances, derogatory comments against the borrower, defaulting a loan without good cause, and negligent disposal of the collateral. Review your lender's conduct. Underscore any questionable lender practices. Let a good lender liability lawyer review your claim. A strong case puts your lender on the defensive.

REFINANCE YOUR WAY OUT OF TROUBLE

Refinancing your property might save your property from foreclosure. Can your equity in your property support new borrowing? A new second mortgage can cover your arrears on a first mortgage. Refinancing your first mortgage may give you enough the money to cover future payments on your new loan until your cash flow improves. Refinancing is a sensible alternative when your negative cash flow is temporary, or when interest rates are lower. Refinancing with a lower interest loan will ease your cash flow.

Will your second mortgage lender help you? Default on your first mortgage and you're in trouble. But so are your secondary lenders. In foreclosure, they must pay the first mortgage, or risk losing their own mortgage. So, second mortgage holders might assist you and themselves by helping you pay your first mortgage. An interim second mortgage is a financial solution when you have temporary cash flow problems and the second mortgage holder foresees no further money will be needed to cover the first mortgage. Offer the second mortgage holder a bonus: Equity in the property? More interest? Faster repayment? Negotiate!

Involve anyone potentially hurt by your foreclosure. What about a key business tenant whose lease could be in jeopardy? If your business faces foreclosure, will a major supplier help? They don't want to lose your business and any money you owe them. Your landlord may help pay your lender, rather than lose that good tenant. When others share your problem, make them part of the solution.

NEGOTIATE
WORKABLE LOAN TERMS

The value of your pledged collateral determines your maximum loan. Secured lenders restructure debt chiefly based upon the collateral's liquidation value, plus whatever recovery is available from the loan's guarantors to negotiate your new deal, and anticipate disagreement about your collateral's liquidation value. The type and condition of the collateral and demand for the collateral make accurate liquidation estimates difficult. Don't forget liquidation costs, auction and attorney's fees and other expenses that will significantly reduce a recovery under a forced liquidation.

Lenders resist renegotiating loans for many reasons. A lender secured by the SBA or another solid guarantor can take a hard position since the lender relies chiefly on the guarantor to secure its loan. Consider your lender's alternatives. Essentially you have four ways to restructure your loan: 1) extend the loan, 2) defer principal payments, 3) reduce the interest, or 4) freeze all loan payments.

Loan workout terms can change. Both you and your lender must be flexible, and constantly reassess the situation for a fair, orderly workout. Lenders strongly resist reducing loan balances and are more willing to extend payments. They eventually want full payment. The optimistic lender hopes your troubled business or distressed real estate may turnaround and that you'll someday fully pay the loan. The time to negotiate a short sale, or "cents-on-the-dollar" settlement, is when the lender sees settlement as better than a forced liquidation that would yield the lender less.

STOP FORECLOSURE WITH BANKRUPTCY

Bankruptcy stops foreclosure. But bankruptcy isn't always your right solution if you only have loan problems. Filing bankruptcy to stop or delay foreclosure is sensible when your property has substantial equity, you need time for a turnaround or to sell the property, or when you want to "cram down" or reduce the mortgage to the property's fair market value. Bankruptcy frequently solves the over-financed property problem, especially when new financing can replace your present loan.

Bankruptcy (Chapters 7, 11 or 13) temporarily stops foreclosure or repossession, but doesn't always prevent it. The lender may get court approval to foreclose if the lender isn't adequately protected. The court imposed delay on foreclosure must not hurt the lender. Your lender would be hurt if the loan balance will increase or fall further behind during the bankruptcy (you don't make interest payments or the collateral decreases in value). The trick is to go into bankruptcy, confident that you can either replace your lender, or keep current on your loan until a long-term resolution can be worked out.

SELL FOR
"NO CASH DOWN"

Here's another great cure for the poor cash flow property. Find a buyer who'll cover the negative cash flow. Who wants such a deal? Someone who'll buy your property for a bargain price, with "no cash down" and can make the loan payments. They want a far bigger long-term gain. The buyer covers the negative cash flow before selling the property. But the buyer may tackle the project if the buyer can cover future losses and sees a big gain at the end.

When facing foreclosure, forget down payments. Your objective is to sell your property before you lose it. Find a reliable buyer. Secure any equity you have with a mortgage against the property. Combine "no cash down" terms with a short sale. Will your lender let you sell the property for less than the mortgage? Will the lender release you from any deficiency on the loan? Be flexible. Don't forget, you and your lender are partners in your "bad loan."

DO AN
OPTION-TO-EQUITY DEAL

Another possible solution when you need more money each month to pay your loan: Suppose your rental property rents for $800 and your mortgage is $1,000 monthly. Cover the $200 deficiency or lose your property. But $800 a month may be the maximum rent from your property *unless* you give your tenant something more than a rental. Try the option-to-equity. It may be your answer. Will your tenant pay $1,000 a month if, in a year or two, your tenant can buy the property and apply the extra $200 a month to the price? You have many ways to structure this. The idea is to give the tenant future ownership in the property. Options-to-equity work particularly well when you have a small cash flow shortage, and your tenant wants to purchase all or part of the leased property. A tenant unable to buy today may be interested in future ownership.

AVOID LOAN DEFICIENCIES. IT CAN COST YOU MORE ASSETS

Foreclosed or repossessed property can cost you more than that one property. You may be liable for any deficiency (the difference between what you owe your lender, including attorneys' costs and fees and what the lender recovers from the sale of the collateral). Lenders sue for a deficiency judgments when can collect. Avoid a deficiency judgment. Offer the lender the return of the collateral without foreclosure. Cooperate. A lender who can avoid the hassles and legal costs of foreclosing, may accept the property rather than chase a deficiency – particularly if the lender knows you're judgment-proof. Also try to find a buyer for the collateral. You'll get a higher price than through foreclosure and may escape a deficiency, or you'll have a smaller deficiency. Avoiding a deficiency is only one goal. Also protect your good credit. Negotiate a release from any deficiency – *and* have your lender agree not to damage your credit. Get those lender concessions in writing.

RECOVER YOUR PROPERTY
AFTER FORECLOSURE

You didn't necessarily lose your property even after your lender forecloses. This is particularly true if the lender repurchased the property. Convince your lender to sell you back your home, auto, boat or other foreclosed asset. Why would a lender sell you back foreclosed property after going to the expense and trouble to foreclose? Here's why. The lender may have anticipated selling the property for more. If the sales price fell far short, the lender may re-sell you your property for the note balance or less. Or the lender may now also see you as a better credit risk, especially if the foreclosure eliminated other liens against the property; you filed bankruptcy or otherwise cleared your other debts. Also, your lender may want to quickly dispose of the property to avoid further costs or liability from holding the property.

In most states, a borrower can redeem autos, boats, or planes after repossession. You can then reinstate your loan and reclaim your vehicle by paying any overdue installments, late fees and legal repossession costs. However, this redemption right is not absolute. You can't reinstate the contract and reclaim your vehicle if you: 1) once had the installment contract reinstated, 2) concealed the property to avoid repossession, 3) damaged or neglected the property, 4) physically interfered with repossession or 5) misrepresented your creditworthiness. Your lender must give you notice of your right to reinstate, or you might reclaim the property even without making overdue payments, but you must punctually pay future installments. To reinstate, notify your lender. If you fail to reinstate the contract or loan within the time stated in the installment agreement (usually 60 to 90 days), the lender can hold you responsible for the loan balance and notify you of their intent to sell the repossessed property. You can then reclaim the property by fully paying the loan.

SHORT SELL
THE PROPERTY

A short sale is simply selling your property for an amount less than the mortgage. Of course, this requires the lender's consent, and lenders naturally resist short sales because it requires them to discount their mortgage and take a loss on the write-down. Still, lenders do approve short sales when it's a practical alternative to foreclosure that may yield the lender a smaller recovery. If you do negotiate a short sale with your lender, also have your lender release you from any deficiency resulting from the short sale. You may incur a tax on the loan forgiveness, so review this with your accountant.

CHAPTER 11

FINANCIAL SELF-DEFENSE IN DIVORCE

Sometimes we must divorce our spouse. But why divorce ourselves from our rightful share of our hard-earned property? Divorce can be an emotionally and economically devastating. Marriage is no longer a lifetime commitment. One in two marriages ends in divorce. Financial self-defense against divorce is then essential whether you're now married, planning marriage or anticipating separation. Unfortunately, most divorces are adversarial. Spouses and their lawyers joust for marital property with nastier battle tactics than in other courtroom feuds. Prepare yourself financially if you must someday divorce.

INSIST ON A
PRE-MARRIAGE AGREEMENT

A pre-marriage agreement is the safest way to protect yourself from a future divorce.

A pre-marriage agreement is a written contract between intended spouses. It specifies how their property and income shall be divided in divorce. Pre-marriage agreements (or pre-marital, pre-nuptial or ante-nuptial agreements) aren't only for the wealthy. *Every* couple needs a pre-marriage agreement. It's their most efficient, equitable way to settle matters in advance of a future divorce. Pre-marriage agreements resolve many issues less easily reconciled by the divorce courts. For example, one spouse may have substantial pre-marital assets and wants his children from a prior marriage to inherit that wealth. A pre-marriage agreement is then the ideal way – perhaps the only certain way – to secure this objective. The pre-marriage agreement similarly guarantees spousal alimony as well as property division upon separation, divorce or death. The agreement lets the parties marry, confident their respective post-marital needs will be fulfilled should the marriage end.

One barrier to the pre-marriage agreement is that intended spouses hesitate to raise the delicate subject of a prenuptial agreement. They fear it communicates distrust, or lack of commitment to the marriage; it is unromantic and too businesslike; it foredooms the marriage to divorce; or it is too expensive. Lovers are optimists. Few believe *their* marriage can fail. Others are unassertive, overly-trusting, or they poorly plan *every* aspect of their lives. Others don't realize how effectively a pre-marriage agreement can protect them from a failed marriage.

It's never too soon to let your prospective spouse know that you want a pre-marriage agreement. The earlier you make this known, the sooner you'll plan your wedding and post-marital finances with less concern.

The greatest benefit of a pre-marriage agreement? It encourages both parties to consider what they really expect and want from their marriage, what the marital relationship will be, and what they expect to give and receive from their spouse. This involves more than finances. For example, an engaged couple may discover that she plans a large family while he wants no children, or the bride may want a lifelong career while the groom assumes his wife will raise their family and not work. The pre-marriage agreement compels you to think about, discuss, and resolve these personal issues. Although a pre-marriage agreement is sensitive, you can soften your request to your intended spouse. Voice concern for your children from a prior marriage. Or claim your lawyers insist upon the agreement. Or approach it by suggesting the pre-marital agreements as part of your estate planning. An estate plans before marrying, in this instance, includes a pre-marriage agreement.

WRITE A POST-NUPTIAL AGREEMENT EVEN IF YOU'RE MARRIED

Most states allow spouses to write *post*-nuptial agreements. Married spouses may want to contractually agree how they'll divide their assets should they later divorce. As with pre-marriage agreements, the enforceability of the post-nuptial agreement requires the agreement to be fair; that both spouses fully understand the agreement; that neither party defrauded the other; and that each party had independent legal counsel.

With the post-nuptial agreement, the spouses divide their assets without the usual acrimony of divorce. The spouses can then continue to accumulate assets confident that those assets will be fairly divided between them, as they agreed, should their marriage end.

DON'T COHABIT WITHOUT
A COHABITATION AGREEMENT

Many couples now live together without marriage. Some want to test their relationship before they marry. Seniors live together because marriage would disqualify Social Security or pension benefits. Others want to avoid the financial responsibility of marriage, or they don't want to commit to the care of an ill partner. More than a few want to avoid the legal and financial complications from marriage – particularly when one party has substantially more wealth.

Cohabitation agreements define the couple's property rights. The agreement designates their separate property before cohabitation, and also provides for the distribution of the assets acquired jointly and singly during their cohabitation. The cohabitation agreement also resolves responsibility for joint obligations, such as leases and other expenses. Cohabitation agreements are as vital for cohabiting same-sex as well as heterosexual couples. Cohabitation agreements are also crucial when one partner has considerably more wealth than the other. The poorer partner then cannot claim that the cohabitation was for the personal care and services of the wealthier partner on the promise of compensation. A cohabitation agreement precisely defines the nature and purpose of the relationship, and whether it includes compensation for services.

DIVORCE-PROOF YOUR ASSETS WITH AN OFFSHORE TRUST

A spouse can put his or her assets beyond the reach of the divorce court with an offshore asset protection trust.

Spouses anticipating divorce can shelter their assets in offshore asset protection trusts. They must disclose the trust assets to the divorce court, but the court cannot recover or divide these assets. Still, that doesn't always assure victory. Divorce courts can award the victimized spouse more U.S.-based assets to compensate for the trust-shielded assets. The court might also give the injured spouse more compensatory alimony or support. Still, the offshore trust can be useful to secure separate property when you have few remaining assets within the United States and your income is too small for the court to even the score through an excessive alimony award. As with other strategies in this book, your offshore trust transfer must be carefully timed and correctly structured. Your trust must also be in a trust jurisdiction that won't enforce U.S. domestic relations orders. An offshore trust shielding your assets might help you bargain for a more equitable divorce agreement. But as with any other divorce-proofing strategy, your goal should be only to prevent yourself from being exploited. You should not exploit or defraud your ex-spouse, or avoid child support.

WATCH YOUR SPOUSE'S HIDDEN ASSETS

Divorcing spouses hide assets. They sell stocks or bonds or withdraw savings and claim they spent or lost the money. Spouses also title assets to straws. Divorce courts severely penalize spouses suspected of this type of unfair conduct, so play fair. You'll come out ahead. Nevertheless, your spouse may be less honest. Protect your marital assets until they are divided by the divorce court. List every asset that you and your spouse own at the first sign of marital trouble. Record serial numbers and other means of identification. Include assets you own individually and jointly. Your attorney can tell you how to secure each asset pending divorce.

Timing is key. Spouses who play "hide and seek" with their assets oftentimes transfer them to offshore privacy havens, camouflage the title of their owned assets, or sell their business interests to friends, family or partners. Fraudulent asset transfers – particularly those involving business interests – are notoriously common in divorce. A defrauded spouse may attempt to find and recover these assets, but the effort may be futile and expensive. Spouses also delay receiving large incomes or inheritances until they divorce. There are countless ways for spouses to waste or deplete assets. If a spouse intentionally depletes marital assets, the divorce court can set-off the depleted amount against whatever property would otherwise be awarded that spouse.

Spouses most often cheated in divorce are nearly always those who know too little about the family finances. Divorcing spouses don't always honestly disclose their assets. You won't be as easily victimized if you stay involved in your spouse's business interests and finances during the marriage. It prevents a major asset concealment that can only victimize you. Watch your ex-spouse's finances after you divorce. Your ex-spouse may then reveal previously concealed assets.

CO-CONTROL
THE MARITAL ASSETS

A common, simple asset protection strategy is to title marital assets to the less-vulnerable spouse. The obvious problem here is that the spouse who controls the assets can sell, encumber or conceal them. Titling marital assets to one spouse is usually poor planning. Spouses should jointly control the marital assets, for example, as tenants-by-the-entirety or as general partners in a family limited partnership. If only one spouse holds title to the assets, the other spouse should encumber or escrow the assets to some third-party, or to a nominee entity that he or she controls. This prevents the sale or disposition of the property without the non-controlling spouse's knowledge or consent.

KEEP YOUR
GOOD CREDIT

Good credit is one asset you must diligently protect during divorce. You'll lose your good credit if your spouse runs up huge bills on your charge accounts and credit cards. It's difficult to financially cope during the turmoil and expense of divorce, but three timely steps can protect you from losing your good credit.

First, immediately notify your creditors that you will no longer be responsible for your spouse's debts. Secondly, destroy and revoke all credit cards on which you have liability. Don't assume you're not responsible for your spouse's credit card debts. You probably guaranteed these credit obligations. Finally, publicly disclaim liability responsibility for your spouse's future debts. Most states consider public notice sufficient to inform third parties that you reject liability for future debts incurred by a spouse. Check your state laws. Also, accept your own credit responsibilities. If you can't punctually meet your obligations during your divorce, tell your creditors before you default. Let your creditors know the reason for your financial problems, but make small, timely installment payments to show good faith. Most importantly, request that your creditors not to report your defaults to the credit bureau.

SAFEGUARD COMMUNITY AND SEPARATE PROPERTY

The nine community property states view marriage as an equal business partnership. Community property laws thus divide property into community property or separate property. Community property is property acquired jointly or individually during the marriage and used in furtherance of the marriage. Separate property can be: 1) property one spouse owned before the marriage and retains title to after the marriage or 2) property a spouse receives as a gift or inheritance before or during the marriage.

Separate property remains separate property and isn't divided in divorce. If you exchange separate property for another asset, the new property continues as separate property, as do proceeds from the sale. Never commingle separate and joint property. Separate property then becomes divisible joint property. Keep your separate property distinguishable from joint property.

Liabilities that either spouse incurred before marriage also remain separate obligations. While spouses may agree to separately pay certain debts incurred during the marriage, this doesn't bind creditors who can nevertheless collect from either spouse. Marital bills should be either fully paid or indemnified against in divorce.

To protect your property in a community property state, you must list your separate property when you marry. Your spouse must formally agree that this will remain your separate property thereafter. Keep gifts or inheritances received during the marriage separate. These assets will remain free from a spousal claim. Community and separate property can both be subject to creditor claims. You must protect both.

PROTECT COMMUNITY PROPERTY WITH TRANSMUTATION AGREEMENTS

If you live in a community property state, then pay attention to your community/separate property laws. A transmutation agreement can convert community property into separate property and vice versa. A transmutation agreement essentially says that "this specified property – and any property that I acquire hereafter is mine alone and (that) property – and any property that you hereinafter acquire is yours." The agreement divides present community assets, as well as each spouse's future assets, into separate property. Each spouse's creditors then have recourse only to the separate assets of that debtor-spouse. This is far safer than having creditors seize co-owned community property. Transforming community assets into separate assets while you have an *existing* creditor can be a fraudulent transfer. A *present* creditor can claim assets fraudulently transferred to the non-debtor-spouse as separate property. Timing is critical. Prepare your transmutation agreements *before* you incur liabilities. And record the transmutation agreement in the public registry to prove the date of your agreement and that it is still in force.

CHAPTER 12

FINANCIAL SELF-DEFENSE AGAINST THE IRS

Thoughts of the IRS can give anyone nightmares about losing their home, savings, business and other hard-earned possessions. It happens to thousands of Americans every year. Few threats to your financial future are as serious as IRS problems because the IRS has awesome collection powers. On the brighter side; most taxpayers resolve their IRS problems. It may cost them some money, but they survive. IRS collection agents are tough (they have a tough job), but most are reasonable if you cooperate. The IRS has powerful laws to help enforce collection, but as a taxpayer you too have rights. And there are strategies to protect yourself. Understand and assert your rights. It's your first-line of defense against the IRS.

DON'T AVOID
YOUR IRS PROBLEMS

Stonewalling is never your answer when you owe the IRS. The IRS will find you. Its powerful computers are linked to state computers, Social Security and every other federal agency, state tax agencies, motor vehicle departments, unemployment offices, public welfare agencies, professional licensing boards and voter registration records. Despite their vast informational network, the IRS computers work slowly. It can take years for the IRS to find and come after delinquent taxpayers. Dodging the IRS forestalls the day of reckoning, but few taxpayers forever avoid it. Do you owe back taxes or tax returns? Resolve it with the IRS now! Delay will only cost you more interest, penalties, and mental unrest.

HIRE TAX
RESOLUTION PROS

CPAs, attorneys and enrolled agents (EAs) each represent taxpayers before the IRS. But there's one major difference between these professionals, What you tell your accountant or EA is not privileged. The IRS can subpoena your records from your accountant or EA. However, what you tell your attorney is privileged. The IRS can't make your attorney disclose confidential communication without your permission. You can thus confide in your attorney without fear of disclosure.

If you do retain an accountant or EA, have them hired through your tax attorney or family lawyer. Representing you through your lawyer will make your communications to them as protected as communication to your lawyer.

A growing number of tax resolution firms advertise their services. Some are good; others less so. But do more than choose the right firm. You also need the *right* professional within the firm to represent you. Get references. If you have a major tax problem or violated tax laws, hire a tax professional *before* you deal with the IRS. Never represent yourself.

DON'T RISK MARITAL ASSETS. FILE SEPARATE TAX RETURNS

You'll pay less tax when you file jointly. The trade-off: The IRS can then collect the taxes from either spouse. File individually and you separate your tax liability. Your spouse can then become a safe harbor for the marital assets should you run into tax troubles! A danger with joint tax returns is that you can't easily protect the marital assets, because neither spouse can be that safe harbor. Spouses should *absolutely* file separate returns: 1) when one spouse has chronic tax problems, continuing audits, major tax liabilities or hasn't filed past returns, 2) one spouse faces civil or criminal tax problems, 3) one spouse owns most of the marital assets, and the other spouse has the greater tax exposure, or 4) the marriage is unstable and a divorce probable.

A spouse might be relieved of the tax interest and penalties on a joint tax return in one of three ways: 1) Innocent Spouse Relief, 2) Separation of Liability Relief or 3) Equitable Relief. For Innocent Spouse Relief, Separation of Liability Relief or Equitable Relief, you must request relief no later than two years after the IRS first tries to collect the tax from you. You must also show that when you signed the joint return, you neither knew, nor had reason to know, that there was an understatement of taxes;

that it would be unfair to hold you liable for the understatement of tax; and that you and your spouse (or former spouse) didn't fraudulently transfer property to one another.

"Separation of liability" can relieve you of responsibility for your spouse's (or former spouse's) share of the tax, interest and penalties. You allocate (separate) the understatement of tax, plus interest and penalties on your joint return between you and your spouse (or former spouse). The understated tax allocated to you is generally what you'll pay. This is available only for unpaid liabilities from understated taxes, and refunds aren't allowed. If you do not qualify for innocent spouse relief or separation of liability, you may still be relieved of responsibility for tax, interest and penalties through "equitable relief" if you can convince the IRS that it would be unfair to hold you liable for unpaid assessments on your joint return. The point: If your spouse – or ex-spouse – ran up that huge tax bill, you might have that opportunity to avoid that liability.

ABATE THOSE
HUGE TAX PENALTIES

Few taxpayers realize how frequently the IRS cancels penalties. You can request an abatement of penalties if you can pay the tax liability, but think you should be excused from penalties for good cause. The IRS will waive the penalties if you can show you acted reasonably and in good faith (about 40% of abatement requests are granted). You have good cause to abate penalties if your tax problems were due to illness, destroyed records, family problems (divorce or death in the family), improper advice from a tax professional, or erroneous written advice from the IRS, war, dishonest bookkeepers, alcoholism, drug addiction, bad business decisions – even that you simply forgot to file. Non-compliance abatements include civil fraud penalties, negligence penalties, penalty for failure to pay estimated tax, failure to file penalties, late filing penalties and dishonored check penalties. If you have reason to abate, send the IRS a signed request for the IRS to remove the penalty and explain your reasons (include specific dates, names, amounts, locations, etc.). Provide documents to support your case. Include your name, Social Security number or employer identification number, the penalty and type tax and years for which you owe the penalties. The IRS will let you know whether they accept your explanation as "reasonable cause" to remove or reduce your penalty.

NEGOTIATE INSTALLMENT PAYMENTS

Here's your solution if you owe the IRS more than you can immediately pay, but have enough income to fully pay the tax over a reasonable time. Taxpayers frequently can't handle one huge tax bill. With installment agreements, you make partial payments of your tax liability in manageable amounts, generally monthly. Your installment agreement is based on how much you owe, your ability to pay, and the time the IRS still has to collect the tax from you. If the IRS agrees to your installment agreement, they'll probably file a tax lien along with the installment agreement. An installment agreement doesn't stop interest and penalties.

Before you enter into an installment agreement, consider less costly alternatives – such as a bank loan or an IRS Offer in Compromise. If you file your returns and can't fully pay the IRS, attach installment agreement Form 9465 to your return. Indicate how much you can pay each month. IRS procedures vary based on the amount in question, and there are now simplified procedures (when you owe less than $10,000); and more complex requirements when you owe over $25,000. Most tax problems are resolved through installment agreements. The IRS will expect monthly installments at least equal to the monthly difference between the taxpayer's income and allowable expenses. If both spouses work and only one has the liability, the IRS will expect the spouse with the liability to pay at least the monthly difference between the delinquent spouse's income and their percentage of the total household allowable expenses (usually the percentage this spouse contributes towards the total family income). Installment agreements beyond five years are seldom sensible to the taxpayer. If you owe the IRS more than you can fully pay within five years, then submit an Offer in Compromise (if you have few assets); sell or borrow against your assets to pay the tax, or file bankruptcy.

SETTLE WITH THE IRS FOR PENNIES ON THE DOLLAR

The IRS may accept part payment of your overdue taxed as full payment. The IRS often settles for pennies on the dollar. To negotiate your offer in compromise, you must convince the IRS that your offer will give the IRS more than what they could collect through enforced action over the next five years. Since your offer must exceed what the IRS can gain from seizure of your assets, you must either be asset-poor or asset protected. Your future earnings potential is also a factor. Submit your offer when between jobs or when your future employment earnings are bleak. An offer in compromise effectively reduces your tax liability to what you can afford to pay now and prospectively over the next five years.

The IRS suspends collection while considering your offer if your offer is reasonable and in good faith. When you submit your offer in compromise, you must reveal your assets and income. The offer in compromise also adds one more year plus the time it takes for the IRS to consider your offer to the 10-year collection period. *How to Settle with the IRS...for Pennies on the Dollar* (Garrett Press) explains this and the other IRS strategies. Settle *your* tax bill for pennies on the dollar! Convince the IRS that it's truly *their* best deal!

STAY POOR
FOR TEN YEARS

Installment agreements and offers in compromise is an answer for some taxpayers. But you may have too few assets and too little income to qualify for either. The IRS will then stop their collection efforts against you by declaring you "uncollectable." This is a temporary determination. If your assets or income increases, the IRS can renew collections.

The IRS has ten years from the date of assessment to collect back taxes. That's when the statute of limitations expires. The IRS must then end further collection, unless you waive the statute of limitations. Of course, you should never voluntarily extend the statute of limitations. Once the statute of limitations expires, your IRS problem ends. Extend the collection period and you extend your tax problems. If you qualify for "uncollectible" status, you are a good candidate for an offer in compromise. With an OIC, you'll finally and conclusively solve your tax problems for a surprisingly small amount and then won't have to stay poor for the next ten years.

TIME YOUR BANKRUPTCY
TO DISCHARGE YOUR TAXES

Can bankruptcy end your tax problems? Maybe. It depends upon the type bankruptcy, the type tax you owe, and when you file bankruptcy.

Do you owe personal income taxes or employee withholding taxes from a business? Withholding taxes aren't dischargeable in Chapter 7 bankruptcy. Income taxes are dischargeable in Chapter 7 bankruptcy if they are more than three years old from the due date when you file bankruptcy. Then consider the type bankruptcy. Income taxes – whether more or less than three years old – aren't automatically discharged under Chapter 13 wage-earner plans or Chapter 11 reorganizations. Under Chapter 13, you make monthly payments for three to five years to partly or fully pay your debts. Taxes have priority over other debts, so a tax claim is usually fully paid under Chapter 11 and Chapter 13. Chapter 7 bankruptcy might end your tax problems if your taxes are over three years old from their due date, have been filed for at least two years, and have been assessed at least 240 days. More recent taxes are not dischargeable. You also must not have negotiated an installment plan, submitted an offer in compromise, or had your claim adjudicated in court at least 240 days before filing bankruptcy. Bankruptcy also won't discharge understated taxes or liabilities on false tax returns for the tax years you want discharged. Bankruptcy also won't discharge or release liens previously filed against your property. The bankruptcy court can allow the IRS to seize liened property.

PROTECT YOUR ASSETS
BEFORE YOUR PROPERTY IS LIENED

One way to protect your assets from the IRS is to convey your assets to a safe harbor well before your assets are encumbered by a tax lien. Timing is critical. Transfers after a tax lien is filed against you won't stop the IRS from seizing the liened property. The IRS can also recover fraudulently conveyed property. The IRS often files nominee liens against property transferred fraudulently. The IRS must litigate the transfer, and the IRS may not attempt to recover transferred property unless the tax liability and value of the transferred property is large or the transfer blatantly fraudulent. But this doesn't suggest that you should hastily attempt to put your assets beyond IRS reach. Nor should you do it without professional advice. Stay clear of legal problems.

To safely title your assets against the IRS, you can title your assets to family limited partnerships or limited liability companies. As the general partner or manager, you (or your corporation) can control the partnership property while the major partnership interest can be safely owned by other family members, corporations or trusts as limited partners or members (without decision-making power). Limited partnerships or limited liability companies can also hold real estate, CDs, savings, stocks, bonds, cars and boats. If the IRS proceeds against your partnership of membership interest, the IRS can only get a charging order or the right to your share of distributed profits and share of the net proceeds upon liquidation, events which remain entirely up to the managing general partner.

You can also transfer your assets to an irrevocable offshore trust as well as encumber your property. Can you borrow against your home, your car or your business? Do you owe money to a relative or friend? Can you use the proceeds to pay down other debts or prepay other expenses. There are legal ways to protect assets from IRS seizure. Though there are other possible strategies, there are also pitfalls and dangers. Get advice from an asset protection specialist and tax resolution specialist before you protect your assets or do battle with the IRS. Your goal is to *legally* protect your assets, not violate the law.

ASSERT YOUR TAXPAYER'S RIGHTS

The Taxpayer's Bill of Rights gives you several important rights. In simple English, it explains what the IRS can and cannot do against taxpayers. Order your copy of the Taxpayer's Bill of Rights from your local IRS office. Also get help with your tax problems through the Taxpayer Advocate Service if your tax problems cannot be resolved through normal channels. The Taxpayer Advocate Service is an IRS program that provides an independent system to assure that unresolved tax problems are promptly and fairly handled. Each state and service center has at least one local Taxpayer Advocate, independent of the local IRS office. They report directly to the National Taxpayer Advocate.

NEVER RELY ON
THE EXEMPTION LAWS

"Federal law trumps state law," so the IRS can ignore state exemptions that protect certain assets from other creditors. Furthermore, state law, as well as federal law, often makes allowances for the IRS to attach property that is off-limits to other creditors or even other federal agencies. For example, Texas state law generally protects 100% of wages and 100% of a person's primary personal residence (a.k.a. "homestead") from creditors. However, these exemptions provide zero protection against IRS wage garnishment and federal tax liens. Likewise, even if an IRA, annuity, or life insurance policy is exempt from creditor attachment as a matter of state law, it isn't protected against the IRS. Even federal exemptions, such as the ERISA anti-alienation provision that otherwise provides unassailable protection for certain pension plans, usually won't protect against IRS liens and levies.

Other ways to protect your wealth:

1. Hold assets in LLCs and limited partnerships, as well as (though somewhat less effective) in corporations.

2. Equity strip. (Note that equity stripping of accounts receivables (A/R) is only effective for 45 days after a federal tax lien is placed on the A/R.)

3. Offshore asset protection is an answer, provided that all reporting requirements are met.

4. Non self-settled irrevocable spendthrift trusts is another option.

5. As a last resort, bankruptcy may discharge certain tax claims, except for income tax debts less than three years old.

6. Because state and federal exemptions are generally ineffective against tax collection activity, 401(k), IRA, and other such funds are best protected by investing these funds, to the extent legally possible, in an offshore LLC with a non-U.S. manager. The offshore manager, of course, is not in the jurisdiction of a U.S. court and thus is not required to obey any U.S. court order to hand LLC funds over to the IRS or any other creditor.

In addition to the above strategies, keep in mind that the average IRS collections agent or IRS attorney may not be very skilled at piercing a solid program. At the same time, if the IRS does take you to court, it will be able to use the same remedies that other creditors have to attempt to pierce your structure, such as fraudulent transfer law or an alter-ego argument. The best plans, of course, are reinforced against these creditor remedies and will plan for the (albeit unlikely) possibility that the IRS will litigate their claim.

A word of caution: you must be particularly careful when protecting yourself against the IRS – especially when you have been assessed a tax liability. You don't want to obstruct justice or impede the collection of taxes, which can be criminal offenses. It's vital then to be guided by an attorney who can keep you on the right side of the law!

IT'S COMMITMENT TIME

We wish you well, dear friends.
May the road ahead be smooth.
May the Gods smile upon you and the lawyers ignore you.
And may the wind be ever at your back.

We thought it would be easy to say farewell, but a simple good luck finish gave us a sense of a job not quite complete. And as you can appreciate, it's impossible to cram 45 years experience into one book. At best, we can only give you an overview of some possible ways to protect yourself.

Most importantly, we know that reading a book such as this means nothing unless you act on its advice.

So it's commitment time. Here's what you should do:

1. Visit our website at *www.AssetProtectionAttorneys.com.* You'll get to know us a bit better, and see the many ways we can help you accomplish your financial goals. You'll also find lots of additional information on many topics discussed in this book, as well as many valuable resources.
2. Give us a call. We'd enjoy chatting with you for a few moments. We would particularly appreciate your comments about the book and ideas on how we can improve the next edition. Of course, we would be pleased to more fully explain our services and how we can help you with your planning.

Better still.....

3. Phone us for a full professional consultation. We can easily handle it by phone or at our office in Florida. We'll completely review your situation and give you a specific plan to fortify yourself. Best of all, we'll give you a special courtesy rate of only $250 for this initial consultation (our normal charge is $500 – $1,000). As a bonus, we will also give you a 2-hour Financial Self-Defense seminar DVD. This alone is a $350 value. Plus, we'll enroll you in our Financial Self-Defense on-line newsletter (another $49 value)!

Give us a call. It may be the most important phone call you'll ever make!

P.S. Register today for one of our *Financial Self-Defense* seminars...or webinars.

ABOUT THE AUTHORS

Arnold S. Goldstein, one of America's foremost wealth preservation attorneys, has protected the assets of thousands of individuals, families and organizations. An attorney, professor and author, he has been featured on hundreds of radio and TV shows. Dr. Goldstein's powerful financial self-defense strategies have been revealed on hundreds of radio and TV talk shows (including CNN, CNBC and NBC's *Today Show*), at major seminars and meetings, and in *INC, Fortune, Money, CFO, Entrepreneur, Success, Venture, Business Week, Bottom Line,* and other major business and financial magazines. His other books on wealth protection are best-sellers. A veteran lawyer (Massachusetts and Federal Bars), his Ph.D. is from Northeastern University where he is professor emeritus. He is presently distinguished professor at Lynn University. Dr. Goldstein resides in Florida with his wife Marlene.

Hillel L. Presser, co-founder of Presser/Goldstein LLC has been featured in countless newspapers and magazines such as *Forbes, Sports Illustrated, Robb Report, Houston Chronicle,* and *Los Angeles Times.* He has also been featured on numerous radio and television stations, including *Fox, NBC, ABC,* and *CBS* and profiled in the international press in Canada, Germany, Greece, Ireland, and the United Kingdom. He represents some of today's most notable professional athletes on wealth preservation matters.

INDEX

MORE FINANCIAL SELF-DEFENSE BOOKS FROM GARRETT PRESS:

- So Sue Me!
- Asset Protection: The Professional Advisor's Guide
- How to Settle With the IRS for Pennies on the Dollar
- Offshore Wealth
- The Doctor's Wealth Protection Guide
- The Limited Partnership Book
- How to Protect Your Money Offshore
- About Your Money
- Great Credit – Guaranteed
- Debt Free – Guaranteed
- Turnaround: Revitalizing the Troubled Company
- …and other great titles available from Garrett Press.

QUESTIONS, FREE UPDATES
OR TO CONTACT THE AUTHORS

- With comments about this book...
- For an online financial self-defense newsletter...
- To order other Garrett titles....
- For one of our authors to speak at a seminar or meeting – or to attend a Wealthsaver® Seminar...
- For a confidential, preliminary asset protection consultation...

Call Today 561-953-1050